THE WELL BROKEN HORSE.

TACHYHIPPODAMIA;

OR,

THE NEW SECRET OF TAMING HORSES.

GIVING FULL DIRECTIONS

HOW TO BREAK AND RIDE COLTS; TO TAME THE MOST VICIOUS HORSES AND GENTLE THEM TO ALL KINDS OF VEHICLES OR WORK; TO BREAK THEM OF KICKING OR ANY OTHER BAD TRICKS; TO TEACH THEM ANY KINDS OF TRICKS OR ACTIONS; ETC., ETC.

WITH NUMEROUS VALUABLE RECEIPTS FOR DISEASES OF HORSES, MULES, COWS, ETC.; HOW TO FATTEN HORSES, COWS, ETC., HOW TO TEACH TURKEYS AND ANIMALS TO DANCE, HOW TO TAME DEER, ETC., ETC.

BY

WILLIS J. POWELL.

TO WHICH IS ADDED

THE BREAKING, TRAINING, AND TAMING HORSES.

BY J. S. RAREY.

With Numerous Illustrations.

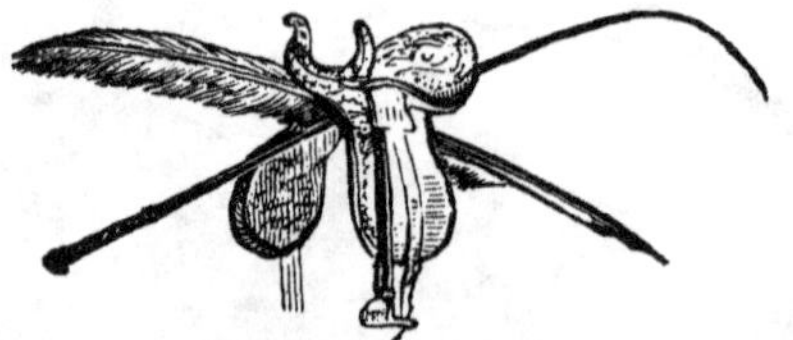

PHILADELPHIA

W. R. CHARTER

611 & 613 SANSOM ST.

1872.

TO THE READER.

Gentle Reader: The work you are going to peruse is not a voluminous one, neither did I take any pains whatever as to the elegance of the style. I wrote to make myself understood by the unlearned as well as the learned. The price of the work may seem high, on account of the small number of pages it contains: but it must be recollected that it encloses the revelation of a secret that has filled thousands of the wise and unwise with astonishment. I have received, as a gratification, more than two thousand dollars, from several Mexican gentleman, for breaking a single horse, in this manner, in their presence. I shall always feel grateful for the kind and generous reception I every where met with, when travelling through their country. From Louisiana to Mexico—from the Californias to Guatemala—and all over the

Mexican states, when I have been travelling, I never asked for lodging without its being immediately granted—I never asked for a meal of victuals and was refused: the proprietor of a private house would feel himself injured, if you should offer him money for receiving you. You may except from this rule some poor Indian, who sometimes will admit of your offer, when you insist on his receiving some trifle; but a wealthy farmer, or one a little at his ease, would spurn the idea of selling his hospitality. I speak of none of their qualities but that of hospitality, which by the by, is a great one, and very much recommended by St. Paul. It is true, I lost nearly twenty thousand dollars, which were deposited in a store, by a revolution: but, in what country is a man's property safe in revolutionary times?

Several Mexican gentleman solicited me to publish this secret in their country, but I constantly refused to do it; for I always intended doing it in my own native country—not doubting but that I should meet with encouragement from my own countrymen. I was always jealous of having the honor of being the first that ever made it known to the world. It is probable that the famous Irish "whisperer," Sullivan, who died in 1810, possessed the same secret, or some other very much like it, as it appears from the astonishing things related of him, concerning what he did upon horses. The reader will, however, observe, that Sullivan lived in a country where horses were raised as they are in England and in the Northern states: that is, among men and familiar to man. But the horses which I have generally had to deal with, (though I have had every kind,) had been running wild, in the plains and woods, for four, five, six and even ten years, and which, during that time, had never had a rope on them. And besides, the horses of New Spain have always been noted for being remarkably fiery and unmanageable. I have gentled a horse in Texas, which, before that day had, in all probability, never seen a man—a stud of eight or nine years of age, as wild as a deer when taken an hour before. I began the operation, and in one hour made him follow me without pulling him by the halter, and little boys got upon him bare-backed, and saddled and rode him about: in a word, he was a gentle horse. Those horses are called in Spanish Mestenos, (pronounced Mestaneyos and not Mustangs.) What makes me think that Sullivan, as well as he that did the same in England a hundred years ago, made use of the same means as I do, is, that when I was now and then breaking a horse, (which generally took me three or four hours, although, as I said above, I have done it even in half an hour, though rarely,) and afterwards went into a town, the people flocked about to see me, saying to their friends, "This is the man that breaks a horse in half an hour." Now the same has been published of Sullivan: most probably they mentioned the shortest space of time he had done it in, for it is likewise said of him, that sometimes he shut himself up with the horse all night.

Sometimes I have met with an extremely wild horse, which seemed to be gentled, as by enchantment, in a few minutes. I have gentled one of this description in ten minutes, so as to lead him, make him follow me everywhere I pleased, and ride him with as great safety as if he had been gentled twenty years before. But this is not a general rule.

The reader is here presented, in the explanation of this secret, with a specimen of the wonderful powers of the tact upon animals, and at the same time, with a moral lesson of patience and gentleness—virtues as necessary to get along through life among men, as they are when used in taming horses; and the exception to the general rule—I mean those that are to be treated with rigor—is not, perhaps, less rare. I am fully persuaded, that almost every class of people will reap some benefit or pleasure from the perusal of these pages. The naturalist sees in it a lesson of Nature itself. The moralist admires in it the display of gentleness, patience and perseverance; and every man who rides a horse may some day or other find some advantage in consulting it.

I have endeavored to render this little work as useful as possible, on three accounts. Firstly, on account of the profits arising from the sale of a useful work; secondly, for the credit one gets as the author of something good; and lastly, on account of the satisfaction every generous mind must feel in becoming useful to his fellow creatures. I have been most generously encouraged by the inhabitants of Attakapas, where I had resided so many years. As soon as I began my subscription they almost universally became subscribers. In the town of St Martinsville, only three or four individuals refused to subscribe. In Opelousas I met with a kind reception from most of the people to whom I presented the list for subscription. At Fausse River, Pointe Coupe, Plaquemine, and down to New Orleans, they almost universally subscribed. I shall always feel grateful for their kind reception. Encouragement is the deepest and dearest debt that a writer can incur.

I never declared myself to be the discoverer of this secret till the year 1824, when I arrived in the Mexican states. I had my reasons for so doing. Never did a people express more surprise and astonishment at any extraordinary event, than the Mexicans did at my first performance on my arrival among them ; and more especially on account of my being a foreigner; for it is well known that the Mexicans, rich and poor, high and low, pride themselves upon being the best horsemen in the world. And I think there is no foreigner that ever travelled among them, and observed them as I have, but will readily agree in ranking them among the first as to agility, skill and elegance, when mounted upon their beautiful Andalusian steeds. If the Mexican ladies are admired by all foreigners for their natural, easy, unaffected, genteel carriage—surpassing, if possible, in that respect, the elegant Louisiana ladies —so does the Mexican, when mounted on a fine Xaral steed, equal, if not surpass, any other rider in the world. For this very reason, I was every where received with the greatest cordiality and applause, for no people knew how to appreciate better than they a discovery of so surprising a nature.

I wish the reader to observe, that in explaining the operation of the secret of gentling a horse, I have always supposed the horse to be one that required the whole secret, in order to be gentled, though a man meets with many that do not require one-third of what I there lay down: but it is better to do too much than too little in this case, so I shall say no more about it here. VALE, YA ES TARDE, BUENAS NOCHES TENGA USTED SENOR CABALLERO.

THE AUTHOR.

CONTENTS.

2

TACHYHIPPODAMIA.

In the year 1811, whilst residing in Georgia, I read an account of a man who lived more than a hundred years ago, who would take any wild horse, and shut himself up with him in a small yard or stable, and at the end of a few hours, come out with the horse perfectly gentle. Nothing was ever known about the means he employed in gentling him, for he died without ever communicating his secret to any one. I always possessed a great share of curiosity: therefore, as well to gratify it as to become useful to myself and others, I made a great many experiments upon young horses, but without success. I ran great risks in these experiments, but the danger, far from discouraging me, animated me the more to make new trials. At the end of the year 1811, I came to Louisiana,

2*

where there were many wild horses. I renewed my experiments. After having met with many difficulties, I discovered a secret in 1814, on my plantation in the Attakapas, by which I broke a horse in three hours. The horse always remained gentle. By the same method, I broke another; but two days after, I found him almost as wild as ever. This perplexed me very much—why one horse should remain gentle and the other not. I broke two more, and undertook a fifth, which I abandoned after several trials. This took place between seven and nine o'clock in the morning. I then thought the application of the secret ought to be varied. Accordingly, after having adopted and rejected a great many ways of applying it, I fell upon one which proved to be the best. At eleven o'clock, I went in again to the horse; but when he saw me, he reared and pitched and kicked in a most terrific manner. I stopped, notwithstanding, stood still a few minutes, and then began the operation, and saw, with pleasure, that at half past four he was perfectly gentle, and always remained so; for I had already discovered this last most important part of the secret—of having them always remain gentle—and I never have revealed it to any living person.

To give an idea of this mode of gentling horses, I will relate a few circumstances of the last mentioned horse. He was going on eight years old, had always run in the prairie since he had been branded, was a stud of a most fiery, ferocious disposition, and had never been roped from the time he had been branded. To get him into the yard where I gentled him, we were obliged to tie his legs and drag him in, and no one durst go into the yard where he was let loose. He ran at any one, when confined in the yard, with as much fury as a lion or tiger would have done, and he used his teeth and fore feet with as much dexterity as if he had been trained up to it from a colt. After I led him out, I let the saddle fall over his heels, girted him tight and cruppered him. Several boys got upon him, rode him about the yard, tied a dry ox-hide to his tail, and rode him out in this manner into the prairie, without his showing the least sign of fear, either at the rattling of the hide, or at any other object he met with in the prairie. The next day, they rode him to the town, in the midst of a great concourse of people; for it was a holiday. He passed among them with as little fear as if he had been raised in the town. When he came home, he followed any one without pulling him by the halter. He let any one handle his feet, and take them up with as much ease as they could those of any plough horse. I declare that, in thus gentling this animal, I made use of no intoxicating beverage, or smell, or any other means whatever, that might tend to stupify him, or diminish his natural vigor or spiritedness in the least: but, on the contrary, horses thus gentled are fit for immediate use, with all their vigor, as they do not become poor and broken down by length of time and bad usage, as it happens with spirited horses gentled in the common way, with much cost and danger. This is not the only advantage of the secret. It enables the most timid man to break a horse, without danger or fear; for it consists in gentling him completely, before you attempt to get on him.

I have broken an immense number of wild horses, in the Mexican provinces, of the most fiery and spirited dispositions; and have certificates from the President, Vice-President, and many of the most respectable citizens of that Republic, who have been eye-witnesses to this performance. In the City of Mexico, General Maison, Captain Hotchkiss and others, strangers, then in Mexico, have seen me perform.

This secret, though simple, requires a clear explanation, and how to be applied according to the three different kinds of horses: for, though a man should discover enough of the secret to break some of the common horses of this country, he still would meet with many, even here, that he could not break, and would completely fail among the high blooded Spanish studs. But, by perfectly knowing the secret, he will find them even easier to be gentled than almost any others.

There are three kinds of wild horses. The first of these appear to fear nothing, and when confined will run at a man with incredible fierceness. The second appear only to fear man. The third class appear to be afraid of every thing they meet with, when separated from the rest of the horses. Many of the Spanish horses belong to the first class, and frequently suffer themselves to be killed before they can be broken in the common way, and yet they are easily gentled by my secret. Now, it is positively necessary to vary the application of the secret according to the disposition of the horse to be gentled; all of which will be clearly and extensively explained in the publication of this work. The work will, besides, contain some few observations upon horses in general, and in what part of the Mexican provinces the best race of horses is to be found, &c., and an easy manner of fattening a horse in a short time. Likewise, the Mexican mode of preventing horses from breaking their bridles—and how to prevent a horse's back from getting sore even on long journeys: all of which I have proved by experience. How to teach a horse, so that in a few days he will not suffer a person dressed in a certain manner to ride him or come near him. To teach one, so that in a few days he will suffer no one to ride him but his master.

At the time I discovered this secret, I was teaching, (and had been for some time,) the public school or college of Attakapas on my plantation, close to the town, and in my own buildings; for the edifice designed for that purpose had been burnt down some time before. I received, besides what each student paid me for board and tuition a compensation for the use of my buildings, as well as the annual pension from the government of the state of Louisiana; and as I taught the Latin and Greek languages, as well as the French, English and Spanish, I had a great number of students, from different parts of the state, and from other states, which rendered my business pretty lucrative. This was one reason why I did not turn my attention at that time to the gain I might expect to reap from this discovery.

In 1815, I met with a man by the name of Thomas Drinnen, who appeared to me rather eccentric in some respects, but an active, intelligent man, and very fond of horses. I told him I had discovered a secret to break them in a few hours. He wanted me to reveal it to him. I told him I would let him know enough of it to astonish the public, if he would go to Attakapas with me; for it was in the time of vacation, and I was on the

Mississippi, on my way home. He said he could not, but would come there some time afterwards, if I would give him some of the ingredients to make trials with where he was then going. I accordingly supplied him with certain materials, (the better to disguise the real secret,) one of which was that callous substance growing upon a horse's fore legs, called the spur; likewise, the sweat taken from under a man's arm was to be used; the sweat of a horse, mare's milk, &c. Said Drennen really believed that these materials were efficacious in gentling a horse. I now declare to the world, that I had heard of some of them, and made use of the others in my experiments, but found them without the least effect.

In 1819, Drinnen came to Attakapas. I never had mentioned to any one that I knew such a secret. On the contrary, I came into Mr. Grigg's inn, then and still existing at St. Martinsville, distant from my (then) plantation a half a mile, pretending to be astonished at what Drinnen was relating concerning horses, and at the same time incredulous, offering him a gratification of one hundred dollars, to see him break one of the wild horses of this country in so short a time. Mr. Gabriel Fuselier told him that he would do the same, if he should succeed in his essay upon any one of the wild horses upon his plantation, which was about two miles from the town. He accepted the offer, and the following day was decided upon for the trial; at which time he performed, and to the satisfaction of every one. But I had given him no further insight into the secret than this first part of it, more to see what impression it would have upon the public, than for any thing else, as my employment and standing in society were such that I did not like to appear before such a multitude of my acquaintances as a horse-breaker. This was, however, a foolish prejudice; for Fulton by the discovery of the means of making a boat advance with more velocity by the application of steam power, was not, on that account, looked upon as a common boatman.

After these experiments of Drinnen, to whom I had communicated so small a part of the secret, I was fully convinced that a large fortune might be made in almost any country with the secret, such as I knew it; and, as I understood the Spanish language, I agreed with Drinnen to go first to Havana and then to New Spain, and take him with me. Accordingly, I sent him to New Orleans, to fit out a small schooner we had bought in Newtown. But he took the fever and died, and I continued my occupations with success for several years, till I had accumulated a handsome property. Shortly after, I became security for several persons, three of whom left me to pay for them: at the the same time, I had been robbed of six thousand three hundred dollars in the city of New Orleans, and had lost one thousand nine hundred dollars upon the steam-boat Teche. As property had fallen to almost nothing, I sacrificed every thing, to pay other people's debts, and in 1824 went by land through Texas to Tamaulipas, where I received a splendid gratification from the governor of the state, Don Bernardo, Gutierrez de Lara, Don Felipe de la Garza, general of division, and from several other gentlemen who were present at a performance which took place in the town and sea-port of Soto la Marina. From thence I went to Mexico with my family, where I performed before the President, Vice President, the Marquis of Vivanco, Count de Regla Y Jala, General Guerrero, and several of the first characters of Mexico, in 1825, in the month of July. Our Envoy, Mr. Joel R. Poinsett, whom I had the honor of knowing personally at that time, can bear witness of the veracity of the signatures of the above-named gentlemen, as well as of their standing, all of whom gave me certificates which I have now in my possession, and some of which I shall publish in this work.

Here must be inserted the following extracts, the originals of which I have in my possession: as

3

a confirmation of which I will first put down Mr. Poinsett's:

LEGATION OF THE UNITED STATES OF AMERICA,
Mexico, November 15th, 1835.

The undersigned, Envoy Extraordinary and Minister Plenipotentiary of the United States of America in Mexico, hereby certifies: that every faith and credit are to be placed in the documents and certificates which have been given in this country to Willis J. Powell, while a resident in these countries. They are signed by gentlemen of the highest respectability; and there is no reason to doubt that he possesses, in an uncommon degree, the art of taming, in an incredible short time, the wildest and most unruly horses.

J. R. POINSETT.

[A true Copy.]

[TRANSLATION.]

Captain General's Office of the South,
MEXICO, July 27th, 1825.

Don Vincente Guerrero to all Gentlemen Governors, Military Commanders, Civil Authorities, and Inhabitants in general of the United Mexican States—Greeting:

GENTLEMEN: The astonishing faculty of Willis J. Powell, in taming wild horses in a few hours, was recommended to me by persons of the highest respectability, and in whom I place entire confidence. They have written to me in his favor, that I might facilitate him to perform in this city. He has verified the same to the entire satisfaction of all the beholders; and having resolved to continue his operations in other parts of the Federation, where he is now about to go, I recommend him, gentlemen, to your favor and protection, not doubting in the least but that you will be highly gratified with the acquaintance of a gentleman who has made a discovery of so much utility, and which, gentlemen, you will know how to appreciate, as persons who desire to encourage all useful improvements, or any thing that may tend to enlighten your fellow citizens: assuring you that I shall be very thankful for whatever kindness or favor you shall have dispensed to this citizen. It is what I expect from your natural goodness. God preserve your lives many years, &c., &c.

VINCENTE GUERRERO.

Certificate of the Marquis of the Mine of Rayas, in the State of Guanajuato, in the Capital City of the same name.

[TRANSLATED FROM THE SPANISH.]

Citizen Willis J. Powell, a naturalist, and native of New York, of whose astonishing dexterity in gentling wild horses in a few hours, I had already been informed, (from several respectable gentlemen, who had been eye-witnesses to the same in the city of Mexico,) arrived in this city on the 20th of the present month. I immediately sent for him, offering him a handsome gratification to give us a proof of his ability. He verified the same by putting it in practice on the 27th, at the mine of Rayas, with a wild colt, chosen on purpose from among the wildest and fiercest of a party of forty of them, which had just arrived there to be gentled for the service of the said mine, in one of the stables of which he began the operation at three quarters past ten in the forenoon: and myself, as well as several other spectators of this performance, were struck with amazement at beholding this horse at two o'clock so gentle, that after having been led around in every direction by the halter, suffered himself to be rode both by men and boys, as well bare-backed as saddled, tightly girted and cruppered—permitting them to get upon him on either side. After a short time, being let loose, he followed any one who went before and motioned to him with gentleness, without pulling him by the halter—proceeding to where several persons were standing without showing any signs of fear at coming up to them, and passing in the midst of them, permitting any one to lift up his feet and handle him with as much ease as they could handle the gentlest plough-horse. Being put into a large yard, he ate with the rest of the wild horses, his companions, and in going a second time to catch him, there was no need of throwing the rope upon him, he letting any one come up before him and put the halter upon him. The third day, he was rode down from the mine to this city, where he was shod all around, standing perfectly still when the blacksmith took up his feet, and never flinching at the stroke of the hammer. Being shod and led out before a great number of people, the servant threw the saddle over his head, then let it fall over his heels and on either side, and under his belly, without frightening him in the least. To the above relation I was an eye-witness, since I was present from the beginning to the end, without any interruption to all the simple and progressive operations used in breaking this fiery, wild and hitherto untameable animal: being astonished above all to see, that in them this dexterous manager made no use of spurs, whip, clamor or exclamation; but, on the contrary, gentleness and caresses were the only means he put in practice to bring, as it were by enchantment to obedience, this wild animal, whose tractability, even at this time, is doubtless much greater than that which is observed in horses of a gentle nature, tamed at the end of a year or more, with much cost, labor and danger, often losing a great part of their natural spirit by the hard usage they undergo whilst one is breaking them—and more especially those of a noble and spirited nature. As a proof of my being present to all herein related, and wishing to encourage such an extraordinary discovery, I sign this declaration, which I make in Guanajuato, capital city of the state of the same name, &c., &c., August 30th, 1825.

THE MARQUIS OF SAN JUAN DE RAYAS.

OBSERVATIONS UPON HORSES IN GENERAL: AND WHAT LED ME TO THE DISCOVERY OF BREAKING THEM IN A SHORT TIME.

The first experiments I made upon wild horses, in order to break them in a shorter time than that usually employed to that end, consisted in the application of different kinds of smells, such as opium, the oil of cummin, assafœtida, that callous substance called the spur which grows upon the inside of a horse's fore-legs, the sweat from a man's arm-pit, mare's milk, &c., &c. Opium has but little effect upon a horse, even if he smells it a considerable time. But of all these substances, no one tends so much to intoxicate, and even sicken, not only a horse but a man, as that taken from the horse when smelled of for any length of time. Any one who may doubt the veracity of what I here assert, can be easily convinced by experience, if he will. In the next place, the sweat from the arm-pit has a tendency to render a horse sleepy, if smelled for an hour or two. Some horses, thus rendered sleepy, can be handled; but on most horses it has no effect, or very little. Now, as I was determined to publish this secret some day or other, in its true light, I never revealed any other till now, but that accompanied with some one of these substances, with certain directions how to apply them. These directions contained enough of the true secret to tame a horse, so as to astonish the most penetrating. Now and then, a horse would remain gentle that had been thus tamed; but five out of ten would become wild again. Whenever I broke one myself, he always remained gentle. Drinnen sincerely thought that some of these substances were necessary to gentle a horse. I solemnly declare, before God and man, that I do not believe that a horse can be tamed, even for a short time, by the application of any of these substances, without applying to him more or less of the true secret; and furthermore: I declare, that all and every one of them are entirely useless, and of no effect. God is my witness, that if ever this secret was known before, I never learnt it from any man; I discovered it myself, and brought it, as I believe, to its greatest perfection.

A horse is gentled. by my secret, in from two to sixteen hours. The time I have most commonly employed, has been from four to six. After my

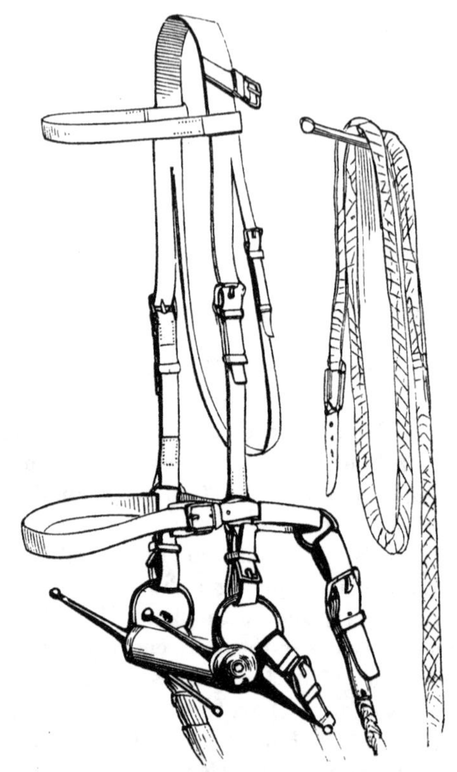

HALTER AND BRIDLE FOR COLTS.

first experiments, I reflected upon the nature of horses in general, many of which, when confined, appeared to fear nothing: notwithstanding this, the result of my reflections was, that fear, much more than any thing else, was the cause of their resistance; of the resistance even of the fiercest; for, although these latter would run at a man, as well as at any other thing, when confined, yet, if they were let loose, and turned out into a field, they would leave him and scamper away. Being once convinced that fear was the only cause of the obstinacy seen in horses taken to be gentled by force, it now remained to discover by what means that fear might be taken away. To take away fear, is, to inspire confidence; or, inspiring confidence, is taking away fear. I believe there is no person, who does not experience a more agreeable sensation, when another person combs his hair, than when he combs it himself. To be vulgar, who is there, that has not found a pleasure in having another rub his legs or arms, hands or feet, if he felt a pain in them, much more than if he rubbed them himself. We all know what pleasure it gives a parrot to have one scratch or rub him upon the head. Now, of the five senses, the sense of feeling possesses something more, as to its influence of materiality, than the other four. It has a similar effect upon animals as upon men. Whereas, the sense of hearing, and that of seeing, have, in many respects, a very different influence upon the human species to what they have upon animals. Animals, in general, are almost or quite insensible to that pleasure, which the human species enjoy, in contemplating beautiful or magnificent objects, though they frequently express great fear at others. They experience the same sensation of fear at sudden or disagreeable sounds, whilst they appear almost insensible to soft and melodious ones. The sense of feeling, in horses, seems to be as exquisite as in men; and in some cases, more so. A horse feels a lively pain at the stroke of a whip, or the prick of a pin. He feels a pleasure in being curried, rubbed and handled. It is well known, that an object that frightens a horse, at first sight, will become familiar to him in a short time—even in a few minutes. The same may be said of those sounds which frighten him at first: such as the explosion of a gun or cannon; to all of which he soon becomes familiar, provided they are not accompanied with any thing that operates upon the sense of feeling; but he will never become familiar to the crack of a whip, so as not to be afraid of it, if he has been accustomed to experience its effects, when vigorously applied to his back. To conclude: Take away FEAR—Inspire CONFIDENCE—FAMILIARIZE.

THE SECRET.

"A GENTLE HAND MAY LEAD THE ELEPHANT BY A HAIR."

Cause your horse to be put into a small yard, stable or room. If in a stable or room, it ought to be a large one, in order to give him more exercise with the halter, before you lead him out. If the horse belongs to that class which appears only to fear man, you must introduce yourself gently into the stable, room or yard where the horse is. He will naturally run from you, and frequently turn his head from you; but you must walk about extremely slow and softly, so that he can see you, and whenever he turns his head towards you, which he never fails to do in a short time, say in a quarter of an hour, or half an hour—I never knew one to be much longer without turning towards me—at the very moment he turns his head, hold out your left hand towards him, and stand perfectly still, keeping your eyes upon the horse, and watching his motions, if he makes any. If the horse does not stir for ten or fifteen minutes, advance as slowly as possible, and without making the least noise, always holding out your left hand, without any other ingredient in it than what nature put in it. The reason of my having made use of certain ingredients before people—such as the sweat from under a man's arm, &c.—was, to disguise the real secret; and Drinnen, as well as several others, believed that the docility to which the horse arrived, in so short a time, was owing to those ingredients. It will be seen, in this explanation of the secret, that they were of no use, whatever; but, by placing so much confidence in them, those who had succeeded in breaking one horse, failed in another, and that is what I foresaw.

No one can accuse me of bad faith, to whom I discovered this or any part of the secret; for I always intended to publish the whole. In the second place, many revealed what I had told them, after the most solemn promise to the contrary. Caution is the parent of safety: I, therefore, by multiplying the ingredients, caused a confusion amongst those who thought they knew the real secret. Though I revealed enough of the secret for a man to break a horse in a few hours, it was not enough to make the horse remain gentle; that is, generally speaking: for some horses would be perfectly gentle ever after; but the greater number would not. The implicit faith placed in these ingredients, though innocent of themselves, became faith without works; and thus men remained always in doubt concerning this important secret. The secret is a complete lesson of morality; for all is GENTLENESS—PATIENCE—PERSEVERANCE.

But, I return to the explanation of the secret. If the horse makes the least motion when you advance towards him, stop and stand perfectly still till he is quiet. Remain a few minutes in this position, and then advance again in the same slow, almost imperceptible manner. Take notice: If the horse stirs, stop without changing your position. It is very uncommon for a horse to stir more than once, after you begin to advance, yet there are exceptions. He generally keeps his eye steadfast on you, till you get nigh enough to touch him upon the forehead. When you are thus near to him, raise slowly, and by degrees, your hand, and let it come in contact with that part just above the nostrils, as lightly as possible. If the horse flinches, (as many will,) repeat with great rapidity those light taps or strokes upon the forehead, going a little further up towards his ears by degrees, and descending with the same rapidity, till he will let you handle his forehead all over. Now let the strokes be repeated with more force over all his forehead, descending by lighter touches to each side of his head, till you can handle that part

4

with equal facility. Then touch, in the same light manner, making your hands and fingers play around the bottom or lower part of the horse's ears, coming down, now and then, to his forehead, which may be looked upon as the helm that governs all the rest. Having succeeded in handling his ears, advance towards the neck with the same precautions, and in the same manner; observing always to augment the force of the strokes, whenever the horse will permit it. Perform the same on both sides of the neck, till he lets you take it in your arms without flinching. Proceed in the same progressive manner to the sides, and then to the back of the horse. Every time the horse shows any uneasiness, return immediately to the forehead, as the true standard, patting him with your hands, and from thence rapidly to where you had already arrived; always gaining ground, a considerable distance further on, every time this happens. The head, ears, neck and body being thus gentled, proceed from the back to the root of the tail. This must be managed with dexterity, as a horse is never to be depended upon that is skittish about the tail. Let your hand fall lightly and rapidly on that part next to the body a minute or two, and then you will begin to give it a slight pull upwards every quarter of a minute. At the same time, you continue this handling of him, augmenting the force of the strokes, as well as the raising of the tail, till you can raise it and handle it with the greatest ease, which commonly happens in a quarter of an hour in most horses; in others almost immediately, and in some much longer. It now remains to handle all his legs. From the tail come back again to the head; handle it well, as likewise the ears, neck, breast, &c., speaking now and then to the horse. Begin, by degrees, to descend to the legs, always ascending and descending, gaining ground every time you descend, till you get to his feet. Talk to the horse in Latin, Greek, French, English or Spanish, or in any other language you please, but let him hear the sound of your voice, which at the beginning of the operation is not quite so necessary, but which I have always done in making him lift up his feet:—"Hold up your foot," "Leve le pied"—"Alza el pie"—"Aron ton poda," &c.; at the same time lift his foot with your hand. He soon becomes familiar with the sounds, and will hold up his foot at command. Then proceed to the hind feet, and go on in the same manner; and, in a short time, the horse will let you lift them, and even take them up in your arms. All this operation is no magnetism, no galvanism. It is merely taking away the fear a horse generally has of a man, and familiarizing him with him, as the horse experiences a certain pleasure from this handling of him. As a striking proof of this assertion, I will relate what I performed in the state of Neuvo Leon, upon a wild boar, taken two days before in the woods, without being wounded. He was shut up in a pen, or kind of cage, and was so furious that he had eaten nothing for thirty hours. When I came to the cage, which was standing in a back yard, he gnashed his teeth, and became enraged, and foamed in a terrible manner. I stood still before him for more than three quarters of an hour. I held a staff in my hand, around the end of which I wrapped a cloth pretty tight, and advanced it, by little and little, towards the head of the boar. He at first tried to catch it in his mouth; but, by continually repeating the trial, I succeeded in touching the bristles of his head. He made some resistance; but, after I had slightly touched his head a dozen times, he stood still. I continued this operation around his head, and then upon his sides, for half an hour, and also upon his belly and back. At the end of an hour, he appeared half asleep, and I passed the staff over him with great facility, till at last, seeing him so easy, I ventured to pass my hand through the grates, and touch him with it; which, so far from irritating him, he seemed to take an uncommon pleasure in being rubbed and scratched. Here, it must be observed, that, instead of giving light strokes or taps with the hand upon this animal, as I do with a horse, I rather scratched and rubbed him; and, in this manner I continued, till I handled him with as much ease as I conld a dog, and even took hold of his tusks. I left him for half an hour, and when I came back, he was eating corn, for the first time since he had been caught. He appeared to have been about two years old. In the afternoon, I handled him again, for some time; and, finding him so extremely gentle, I ventured to take him out of the cage into the yard, though with the precaution of tying a rope about his neck, in case of his becoming refractory. Before I took him out, however, I made my servant and two or three Indian boys handle him. This last precaution was useless, as he followed me into the house, and ate corn out of my hand. I caused him to be handled and fed that evening and the next morning, when he was finally turned loose among the pigs. This was in the year 1825. I came away the next day, and heard no more of him, and have never had a second trial upon that kind of animals.

To return, again, to the horse, which we left already familiarized to man. Supposing him, as I said in the beginning, to belong to that class which only fears man, or has little fear of any thing else: the horse is gentle, in doing which you may have employed two or three hours; but he has no knowledge of being led by the halter. Put the halter on him, and handle him in the forehead, and pull him gently round towards the left, forming a circle. Let him follow you several times round in this way, till he will go as fast as you wish him to go. Then change the position, and turn to the right in the same manner, talking to him, telling him to come along, &c. When he is familiar with forming a circle, make him leave it; and, by degrees, he will follow you in a straight direction. In all this operation stop him every now and then, and handle his head and all his body, &c. When he is following you, stop him short, always speaking to him, as likewise when you start him: "Come on"—"follow me"—"come along." In a short time, he will follow you without your pulling him by the halter. The first impression is so great upon horses, that a horse broken in this manner will always follow well ever after. Now take a whip, crack it at him, and drive him from you, but without whipping him. Then go up to him, and handle him and caress him, taking his head in your arms, putting your arms around his neck, &c. Finally: Take away the fear he had of you at first. The next operation is to saddle him, which is done almost immediately, if he belongs to the second class of horses, which fear very little else than man; and as he will make no resistance at being saddled, he will make none at being ridden, and so your horse is broken.

I shall now explain the difference to be observed in gentling the third class; that is: those horses which appear to fear every thing. The operation is to be carried on, as above directed, till you come to that part where you are to saddle him. If you should undertake to put the saddle on a horse of this latter description, he would fly from you as quickly as a deer, although you might handle him with the greatest ease. How shall we then proceed? Take away the fear he has of different objects, by making him acquainted with them, and convincing him, as it were, by gentle means, that those objects he so much dreads will not hurt him. Familiarize him with them. In order to succeed in this, every thing must be done by gradation. Firstly: Take a handkerchief and move it gently before him; at the same time, you handle his forehead; make him smell it; toss it up a little in your hand before him, till he is not frightened at it. Then throw it upon his head, and over his ears: then, by degrees, upon his neck, and so continue on; for if you should throw it immediately from his head to his back, or on his sides, he would jump and kick with all his might. Throw it upon his back, and upon his sides; let it fall off on one side, and then on the other. Let it fall before him and behind him, so that it will fall upon his heels. Make him walk with it upon his back. Let it fall whilst he is walking, till he gets completely familiar with it. After this, take some one or two yards of heavy stuff, such as cotton bagging or the like, throw it down at a distance two or three times; then make him smell it. Throw it up before him till he no longer flinches at it; then over his head, always talking to him, from time to time, and handling him every now and then. Then throw it upon his back, whilst you hold it in your hand, till you see that you can throw it upon his back, and let it hang down upon each side, without frightening him. Let him walk round with it: then make him trot with it, till it falls off. Pick it up and throw it upon him as he stands, and let it fall off on both sides of him, under his belly. Let it fall off from behind, over his heels. Repeat this last operation a great many times, and lift up his tail and pull it smartly. Tie something light to it, that will hang down over his hams; but not so low as to touch the ground. Make him follow you, in this manner. Afterwards, tie a large piece of mat or something similar to it, so that it will touch and drag upon the ground. Touch him and handle him in the forehead, making him advance slowly at first, then faster, till you make him run with it, and go around in every direction, till he becomes perfectly familiar with the object tied to his tail. Drive the horse away from you. Then call him back again. Untie the mat from his tail, and tie it to his neck, letting it hang down on one side, and making him run in the same manner as before. Take it off. Take a rattling, dry deer-skin or ox-hide, and throw it down at some distance before the horse. Raise it up and throw it down several times, till the horse pays no attention to it when it falls, or when you let it fall and rattle it. Let it fall close before him, and make him smell of it. Then throw it upon his neck. Let him first walk and then run with it, till it falls off. Then continue with it, as you did with the mat, till you tie it to his tail, and let him walk and run with it, without showing the least signs of fear, which he will do in a very few minutes. Next comes the girt. To familiarize him to it, you will take, firstly, a common rope, and throw it over his back, and make him walk with it. Stop him, and double the rope. Let the middle of it hang upon the right side, low enough for you to take it in your hand where it is doubled, and draw it towards you. Slip the two ends of the rope through the doubled part, and haul it gently and by degrees, as if you were girting the horse. Loosen and tighten it many times; at last, fasten it, not very tight. Make him walk and run in this manner. Loosen and tighten it again, till you have him girted up with the rope in this manner. Walk and run him in this way. Stop him. Throw another rope around his body, just before his hind legs, so as to encompass his flanks. At first, let it rub him gently, and by drawing first one end and then the other. This is very important, especially if the horse be naturally of a fearful, timid nature. The effect it has upon him, ever after, is truly astonishing. I speak after more than twenty years' experience, having done every thing as above directed. Take a heavy Spanish saddle, with wooden stirrups, if you have such a one. Throw it down before him, rattle it well, and make him smell of it. It must be observed, that in all these manœuvres, you must now and then handle the horse, by taking up his feet, speaking to him, patting him all over on both sides pretty vigorously; going away from him, then running suddenly up to him, &c.

To return to the saddle. Throw it up towards his back; and if he makes no resistance, as it is probable he will not, throw it upon his back and girt it lightly. Handle him in every part. Strike first lightly, then very hard upon the saddle: walk him and run him with it. Stop him, and girt up tight. Pull upon the stirrups, on both sides. Make a noise upon the saddle, by striking it hard with your hand. Handle his tail, by raising it and letting it fall, and striking upon it; then put a small cord under it, in form of a crupper, and tie the ends to the hinder part of the saddle. Walk and run him, &c. Pull the cord that serves as a crupper, till he gets familiar with it. Unsaddle: saddle up again immediately. Put on the crupper: girt up tight. Exercise the horse, by leading him, and making him run. Stop him all at once. Put your hand on his forehead. Say to him, "Come along:" at the same time advance, and pull him gently by the rope. In a short time, you may let the rope fall, and he will stop at the word "Stop," and will follow you, at the words, "Come along," without your pulling him by the rope. Now ungirt the saddle, and let it fall down upon the left side. Put it loose upon the horse again, and let it fall several times upon the right side and over his heels. Then take it and throw it over his head, upon his back; saddle him roughly, striking and making a noise upon the saddle. Pull the stirrups strongly, and lead him about. Load him with any baggage that comes in your way, and make him walk and run with it. Mount half way upon him, bearing hard with your left foot upon the stirrup: then upon the other side. If the horse shows no signs of fear at any of these operations, you may get upon him with all safety, and ride him through the most populous city in America, without his being frightened at any of the objects he meets in it. But I generally make it a rule, to accustom the horse to sound, before I take him out: in order to do which, I take something that is similar to a drum, or an empty barrel, and beat upon it till he becomes perfectly indifferent to it. Then I show him a pistol or a gun, and flash it before him. Then I load it very lightly, and fire it off before him, close to his head, making him smell it before I fire. I flash it off two or three times before-hand. I load it again, and by repeating this exercise two or three times, you may fire off the gun while placed upon his neck, without frightening him in the least.

I have already observed, that the first impressions are the strongest and most lasting. It is a great deal easier to learn, than to unlearn. Therefore, it is extremely necessary, that the horse should be exercised in every thing that tends to render him docile and useful, when you thus break him, and you will have very little to fear from him afterwards. After you have thus gentled your horse, so as to be able to ride him, it will be necessary for you to come up to him with one or two other persons: let them touch him, and let him smell at them: otherwise, he would be afraid of other people: but, by coming up to him with other

THE HORSE WITH LEG STRAP AND SURCINGLE ON.

persons, he will let any one handle him and manage him, as easily as the one who broke him. The greater part of wild horses thus gentled, will go off with facility: others will be a little awkward at first. It is, perhaps, the best way, (though I have generally ridden them out alone,) and especially if they show any awkwardness in going at first, to ride them out in company with another horse. It will do no hurt to any. Horses broken in this way, become almost immediately bridle-wise, and need but very little exercise, to obey the bridle with uncommon facility. The reason is plain: they are no longer afraid, and consequently have no inclination to resist.

Having thus shown how one must proceed, to break the second and third class of horses, I now retrocede to the first class, which appear to fear nothing. When this first kind of horses are let loose, after having been dragged by force into a pen or stable, it is very dangerous for any one to go in where they are; for, if you step back or try to get out of their way, when they run at you, they will be sure to bite, kick or stamp you under their feet. But if you stop, stand perfectly still, hold out your left hand, and look at the horse, he will stand still, likewise, before he arrives at where you are. This may appear very strange; but so it is, and I have experienced it very often. He will never come nigher than about five or six feet to you; and if he is in a yard, he will rarely come nigher than ten or twelve. Such a horse should never be put into too small a place. Here we must make use of a precaution, which is not necessary in the two other kinds of horses: and give me leave to say, that I am fully persuaded, that no horse of this description was ever gentled in a few hours by any one but myself, and by the secret which I had discovered. The precaution I speak of, is: to let no one come into the stable or yard with you, for it would be dangerous. His attention must be fixed upon you, and your hand alone. I once came near being killed, by a horse of this description, before I had discovered this part of the secret. Therefore, it is of the greatest importance, to put the horse where he can see no moving object, at the time you approach him. The case I mentioned was this: I was about to draw nigh the horse, after having entered the stable where he was, and after he had stood still some time, when, on a sudden, a hen flew down from a scaffold exactly over the stable where the horse stood, and where I was to perform the operation. The horse gave a jump at me, and struck his foot so nigh me, that he grazed my shoulder; then turned round almost as quick as lightning, and let fly a pair of heels, which knocked off my hat, but knocked a useful lesson into my head. From that day forward, I have never received the slightest hurt, or even run any risk, in breaking some of the fiercest and most ferocious horses of New Spain. But to come to the point. Hold out your left hand, keeping it high enough to touch him upon the forehead: keep this position for at least one whole hour, lowering your hand now and then, unless the horse should advance, after ten or fifteen minutes, a step or two towards you; in which case, let your hand be ready to meet his forehead, rather higher up than in the other two kinds of horses; and, if he should appear uneasy, repeat the strokes very fast between his eyes, fetching your hand partly over them now, and then. Your position, at first, ought to be exactly before him. Then, by degrees, fall off towards the left side. Never flinch, or show any signs of fear, when you are gentling this kind of horses. You must remain a great deal longer about their heads, than in others. They will often flinch, and frequently show signs of resistance, whenever you advance an inch from the place you have already handled; so that it requires some judgment, and more patience, to know how to manage them. But, by going on, after you have once touched them, as you would do with the other two classes, though a great deal slower, you will never fail of making them as gentle as a lamb. I never employed more than ten hours but with one, which belonged to the Governor of San Louis Potosi, Don Jose Ildefonso Leon. This animal kept me between fifteen and sixteen hours, in gentling him; at the end of which time, men, women and children could ride him and handle him with as much ease as they could any old, gentle cart-horse, and ride him bare-backed through the streets of the city, as many did—five or six being mounted upon him at once. For he was a stud of ten years of age, of great strength, of the Arabian race, and very high spirited; and the governor himself, who possessed several thousands of wild horses—and was the best horseman and herdsman in America, always had thought, for the last four years, that it was not in the art of man to break him. He was offered a thousand dollars for him the same day I finished breaking him, by an English gentleman, by the name of Humstead, who was travelling through the country: a great price, in a country where you can get a good horse for thirty or forty dollars. I would always advise a man, that goes to break a horse, to have a watch with him; for the time will always appear long to him, when he undertakes a horse of this description. It is very uncommon to meet with a horse you cannot come up to, so as to touch him in the forehead with your left hand, in less than a half a quarter of an hour.

Now, any person who may in the least doubt of his own capacity to perform the operation, according to the rules laid down here, can always have a halter, or what the Spaniards call a jaguima, (which is generally used in riding young horses, before the bridle is put on them,) put upon the wild horse, before he is let loose, with a long rope tied to it, dragging upon the ground. When he goes in to the horse thus haltered, he will take care to take the rope up gently in one hand, whilst he holds out the other; taking care that the rope may keep clear of all his feet, and lie before him, gathering it up as he approaches. Another precaution may likewise be used, by persons naturally afraid of horses, which is: to have a barrier placed between them and the horse, and the end of the rope on the side they stand, which they may take hold of, and proceed as above directed. The barrier, if made use of, must be open enough for the horse to have a full view of the person who is going to break him. It is always a considerable inconvenience; but, it has this advantage: it places the most timid out of the reach of all the harm he might fear from horses of this description, till he can handle their head, which is already a great point; but, as one can handle but a small part of the horse, in this manner, it is necessary to go in to him afterwards, when he is thus a little familiarized to you; for there is no danger, after you once handle his head, if you proceed according to the above directions; that is, always advancing by degrees. Whenever you can handle the horse in every part, you must handle him much more vigorously than at first, though without hurting him. Those horses which appear to fear nothing, but kick at every thing with a kind of spite, and run at men when confined in a close place, are not always the longest in becoming perfectly gentle. Though a man may sometimes be an hour before he can touch them, yet they frequently become reconciled to him, as soon as he can handle their head, and it is not unfrequent to see them very easy to be saddled and ridden, and more especially if they have never been handled; because a horse that has once been taken, in order to be broken the common way, and has resisted with success; that is to say, has flung his rider and run away—or one that has been beaten, whipped, or badly used in any way, is a great deal worse than one that has never been touched; for it is more difficult to unlearn than to learn. It is necessary always to bear in mind, what I have said concerning first impressions.

To conclude: To which soever of the three classes horses belong, deal with them as with the third class; that is, those that fear every thing, with this difference: the first class, or those that appear to fear nothing, must not be approached so suddenly as the others. Take notice: Whenever a horse that you begin to handle, hangs down his head, or appears sleepy and careless, (and this will happen in some in less than an hour,) your business is half over. I have broken an extremely wild horse, so as to saddle him, bridle him, and make him follow me without pulling him by the halter, and so that men, women and children have ridden him, without the least danger, in the streets of one of the most populous towns of the United Mexican states: and this I have done in less than two hours from the time I went into the place where the horse was. I always carried a watch with me, when I broke a horse. I have now and then gentled one, so as to ride him with perfect safety, in less than one hour. However, these are rare cases. I never had but two that kept me ten hours, and one nearly fifteen hours and a half. I began him at two o'clock, and worked upon him till seven; and the next day I began at five, and finished him a little after one o'clock. This was the Governor of San Louis Potosi's, and one of the highest spirited horses I ever saw. I have generally employed from four to six hours, and some times eight, in rendering a horse completely gentle and useful, and on which a man or woman might undertake a journey of a thousand miles, the very next day after being broken, without any kind of fear of his becoming refractory on the road.

To come now to the most important part of the secret. I observed, in the beginning of my discourse upon the experiments I had made, that I was surprised to find one of the horses I had gentled the day before, almost as wild as ever, and one of the others had remained perfectly gentle. I saw there was something lacking. I therefore broke another; and, after having finished, I tied him in a stable. I went to him at night, and made a little negro boy handle him a quarter of an hour: gave him half a spoonful of fine salt, and not more than about half as much as he would eat. Early in the morning, I went to him again, handled him in the forehead and all over, and took up his feet, &c., &c., for a quarter of an hour: took him to water; fetched him back; gave him another spoonful of fine salt, and plenty to eat afterwards. I rode him a couple of miles, and then let him loose. The next day, I caught him in the yard, amongst the other horses, without throwing the rope, and he remained gentle ever after. The first day you break a horse, it is always good to ride him two or three miles; if further, it will do him no hurt. The first time you ride him out, it will be well enough to accompany him with another horse, though this is not absolutely necessary; for many horses, especially high spirited ones, will often go as well as if they had been gentled for a long time; some others appear a little awkward at first, but in half an hour they will go well alone. At any rate, they will not be afraid of any object they meet.

I have here given the whole secret of taming, in a few hours, the most refractory wild horse.

Whilst residing in the city of Mexico, I wrote a grammar, in Greek, Latin, French and English, which I intend to publish, in order to simplify, in some measure, the study of the former. In it I begin by making the student acquainted with the most common names—such as fall under his immediate view. The names of birds, fish, plants, trees, the human body and its parts, &c., &c. In the declination of all these, will be found general rules; but all, or almost all of these rules, are subject to some one or more exceptions—as is the case with all general rules. Thence, perhaps, came our proverb: There is no rule without exception. Now, as gentling a horse, and writing a grammar, are two very different occupations, yet they have some things which are common to both: one of which is, this same exception to the general rule. I have given a detail of the method I use in breaking the three different kinds of horses: that is, horses in general; these general rules, however, are liable to some few exceptions. I have had horses that did not appear to belong to any one of the three kinds mentioned. I look upon them as exceptions. Among these, are horses that toss up their heads the very minute you touch them, and will not let you put your hand upon them. The first of these I met with gave me so much trouble, that I thought it would be impossible to break him. I tried to touch him upon the forehead, as the true standard, but could not. I therefore declared him to be an anomaly, and determined to decline him in some other way. I therefore endeavored to touch him upon the neck, which I succeeded in doing in less than five minutes. I proceeded on in handling him, as I did other horses. After having lifted up his feet, and handled him every where except about his head, I succeeded in gentling that part. He always remained gentle, and not in the least skittish about that part. To succeed in handling his head, I was obliged to begin at that part of the neck nighest to the ears, and continue on to them, and then to the upper part of his forehead, between his eyes; and so descend to his nose, in the same progressive manner as I ascend in other horses. I had tried every possible means to begin at that part, but found it utterly out of my power.

Another exception to the general rule, are those

horses which, after having been begun, and already handled in the forehead, show an inclination to bite, as you proceed on, and would actually do so, without your taking some precaution. Now, as my general rule of gentling horses is all mildness, gentleness, &c., except from this rule horses of this latter description; and, whenever they show an inclination to bite, correct them by giving them a pretty smart slap with your hand, and they will never repeat it more than two or three times. I never knew this to happen with horses of the first description, which one would be naturally inclined to suppose more apt to do so than any others. As to the rest, proceed as in others. If you wish your horse to go in a cart, coach or plow, after having gentled him in this manner, harness him, put on lines, and at first make him go round before you several times: you will tie some light thing behind, for him to drag, and go on progressively, and in a very short time you may harness him to a cart, or plough, and he will go off without difficulty; especially if you do this immediately after having gentled him, for then is the best time to take away all caprices. It is well to give him a few days exercise.

OBSERVATION. If the horse you are going to break has received a blow upon his forehead, his ears, or about any part of his head, so that it is sore or painful when touched, it is useless to undertake to break him before he gets well: for the very touch which would give him pleasure being well, gives him pain in this situation, and the more you try to handle him the more you will irritate him. Let him get well, before you undertake to gentle him.

REFRACTORY HORSES GENTLED FOR A LONG TIME IN THE COMMON WAY.

I begin first with those which are afraid of a gun, or the like. Cause a pen to be made, just big enough to put the horses in, and in such a manner as to be able to go round it in every direction, as well behind as before; and let the bars be far enough apart for you to handle him every where. Let him remain in his pen or cage from two o'clock in the afternoon till the next morning, without eating or drinking. The pen ought to be made so high, that the horse cannot reach his head over it, and with four strong posts in the ground, so that if he should fall back upon the bars, that traverse it behind, his weight will not be sufficient to break or derange them. Go to him in the morning. Handle him smartly a few minutes; then stand at a distance before him, with your gun in your hand, without moving it, but so that he can see it. If he is frightened at it, keep your position for some time, till he remains quiet, then flash it off. Repeat this, till he is in some measure reconciled to it. Draw nigher. Repeat the same: flash it off before him, very nigh. Handle him in the forehead, and hold the gun in one of your hands. Go on thus progressively, till you can load and fire it off over his head, with as heavy a charge as you wish to put in it, which you will be able to do in about two or three hours. When you have gone thus far, run suddenly up to him, with your gun in your hand. Handle him in the forehead, holding it still in your hand. Exercise him well in this way, till he does not flinch or show any signs of fear, when you thus approach him. Now, you suppose the work to be completed? If you do, you are very much mistaken; for you must recollect, that he has much to unlearn. Take away Fear—Inspire Confidence—Familiarize—are three great lessons to be taught, in the art of gentling a wild horse; and, to bring a rebellious horse to obedience, you must add, Unlearn. Repeat the same, unlearn, &c., till he is completely gentle.

Now give your horse a plenty to eat and drink. I suppose it to be about ten o'clock. Let him rest, if he will. Repeat your lessons at four o'clock in the afternoon, more or less rapidly, according as he is inclined to obey them. Feed him at night; let him remain in the pen all night. Next day, go over the same exercise; at the end of which, if you think him sufficiently docile, take him out of the pen, and go through the same exercise that you did whilst he was in the pen. If he shows no signs of fear at the explosion of the gun, when fired off from his back or neck, you are sure of him. But you must exercise him a little, for two or three days more; at the end of which, you may always rely on him afterwards. Should he be somewhat refractory, when you take him out of the pen, which would be a rare case, though some horses may be, put him again into it, and repeat, and you will never fail to succeed. In the same progressive manner, you can correct the defects of a skittish horse, in a great measure; but some are of so fearful a nature that, if they have been gentled in the common way, it requires a great deal of patience to manage them.

A SKITTISH HORSE.

The best method of correcting a horse of this description, when one is on the road, is, to stop him suddenly, whenever he appears to be frightened at any thing he sees before him or at his side. Let him stand perfectly still: get down, if he does not become quiet in three or four minutes, and handle him in the forehead. Lead him by the bridle to the object that frightened him: then lead him back to where he was, and get on him. Ride him up to it, &c. You can likewise give him the same exercise as you do to a wild horse of the third kind, and you will not fail to succeed in correcting him by repeating it several times. I never knew a horse to become skittish that I had gentled by my secret, though I am not certain that such a thing might not happen; for, as I said before, there is no rule without an exception.

A HORSE THAT WILL NOT SUFFER HIS EARS TO BE TOUCHED

Begin at his forehead, just above the nose, and handle it in the same manner as you would do with a wild horse, according to the rules laid down in that part of the secret. Gentleness, Patience, Perseverance, Faith; all these are necessary, in order to succeed with some horses. It has taken me from five to six hours, to be able to handle the ears of some horses; but, at the end of that time, they let me handle them with as much ease as I could those of a house-dog. They will always let you handle them afterwards.

Shortly after my arrival in Mexico, a gentleman who had read an article which the President had caused to be published in the government paper, concerning what I had done with a wild horse that

THE HORSE BOUNDING ON HIS HIND LEGS.

I had gentled in his presence, a few days before, sent for me, telling me he had a horse of great value, that he had given only five hundred dollars for, on account of a defect, or vice, that the horse had contracted two years before, and which had augmented to such a degree, that he would have killed any one that would have attempted to put a bridle on him, or touch him about the ears. He asked me if I thought I could cure him of this evil habit. I told him I would try; and, accordingly, I sent every person away, and went in to the horse. I had taken the precaution of having a halter (jaguima) put upon him before-hand, and a long rope, dragging upon the ground, tied to it. In order to put this halter upon him, they had to throw a rope upon his legs, and tie them, and another around his nose; and this was a ceremony they had to perform every time they put the bridle on him. When I had got in where the horse was, I took up the rope and advanced, holding out my left hand, as when I break a wild horse, and came up to him. I used a great deal of precaution, when I touched him in the forehead for the first time, as I do with a horse belonging to the first class, that is, those that seem to fear nothing; and, continuing on in this manner, gradually ascending, making my fingers play upon his forehead with great rapidity—gaining ground so slow, that I remained two hours before I came to the roots of his ears, which I began to touch very lightly at the end of another half hour; and, by continuing the operation an hour longer, I was able to handle them with ease and safety. A few minutes after, I bridled him, led him about, and made him follow me, without pulling him by the bridle. I took it off, and put it on again. I repeated this exercise several times. Then I called in my servant, and made him bridle and unbridle him. Then sent him to tell the owner of the horse to come and see him.

Give me leave here to observe, that when I performed upon a horse, I never let any one be present, (for fear they might discover the real secret,) except such a gentleman as I knew would give me a handsome gratification: for a man is always more or less willing to pay to satisfy his curiosity as well as his interest.

The owner of the horse came in where he was standing without rope or bridle. I called a little Indian boy, who had never bridled a horse in his life, and gave him the bridle; and, as the horse's head was too high for him to reach up to it, I told him to get into a chair, and put the bridle on. His master cried out, "For God's sake, don't let him go nigh him! I cannot yet have confidence enough in that animal, to let the little boy go nigh him: I know he would kill him, though Beelzebub himself had been to work at him since the time you first went into the stable!" I then went and put on the bridle myself, and took it off; then he agreed to let the little Indian do the same, which he did, as may be supposed, in a very awkward, fumbling manner, standing all the while in a chair, to the great surprise of his master, who then came in and bridled him himself, and made me a present of eight doubloons, (a hundred and twenty-four dollars.)

TO BREAK A HORSE OF KICKING.

Handle the kicking horse in the forehead, and from thence every where, except his legs and feet. Then tie up one of his fore legs, (no matter which); handle him gently all over, and descend, by degrees to his feet, always speaking to him: he will let you handle them in a few minutes. Untie his fore leg, and go through the same ceremony. After repeating this operation two or three times, he will let any one handle his feet with the greatest ease imaginable.

HOW TO MANAGE A HORSE THAT KICKS UP, SO AS TO BREAK HIM OF THAT VICIOUS HABIT.

A horse that is apt to kick up, ought to be dealt with in the following manner: Put upon him a pack-saddle, if you have one; if not, something as nigh to it as possible. Take two bags, and put one hundred and twenty-five pounds of sand in each, if your horse is a common sized one Girt them on, or bind them very tight, in such a manner that no effort of the horse can throw them off. Have another horse prepared at hand, and some one mounted on him to take hold of the rope of the vicious horse, the moment he is loaded with the sand. Let him start off, with another horseman behind with a good whip in his hand; and the more he kicks up, let him whip him the more; or, in other words, let him whip him every time he kicks up. Let him trot off thus, about ten or fifteen miles; at the end of which, take off his load, and let some one get immediately upon him, and trot back with the same speed. After having exercised him thus, for two or three times, it is not common that a horse will ever kick up again.

It is to be observed, that if the horse should kick up with the load of sand at the end of ten miles or more, make him go at least three miles after he has ceased kicking up; but it is very uncommon for a horse to kick up, after the first three or four miles. If he should appear a little tired, you can regulate the distance, more or less, and vice versa. I believe this to be the most infallible remedy known, without exposing one's self. There are other remedies, which none but a good horseman can put in practice; but I write for every class of men that ride on horseback, whether doctors, lawyers or priests, farmers or merchants. If this advice should save a few necks from getting broken, I shall feel gratified.

TO HANDLE A HORSE'S FEET THAT IS APT TO KICK

Put him in a pen, and go on progressively, till you can handle all his feet as you would a dog's. It must be recollected, that when I speak of putting a horse in a pen, I suppose them to be of the most refractory kind imaginable; otherwise, I can handle a bad horse's feet, in a very few minutes, by beginning at his forehead, and so on.

TO TEACH A HORSE, SO THAT HE WILL NOT LET A PERSON DRESSED IN A CERTAIN MANNER COME NIGH HIM.

If you would not wish to have a person, for example, wearing a white hat, come nigh your horse, put on a white hat, go into the stable where your horse is, and take a whip in your hand: go up to him, and give him a few good lashes with it. Retire and change your hat for one of another color: leave your whip, come in again without it; stroke your horse, pat him, talk to him and feed him. Go out again, and put on your white hat: come in and whip him soundly. Then retire, put on another hat, and come in and handle him gently. Repeat the same for a few days, and your horse would as lief see the devil as a man with a white hat, and will not let such a one come near him; and thus it will happen with any other clothing.

I will relate a little anecdote, which took place in Mexico, a few years before I left there. One of my friends had a horse extremely gentle, and of such an easy, agreeable gait, that he took the greatest care of him, and held him at a great price.

A well-fed, big and lusty friar was a friend to our neighbor: one who liked the good things of this world, as well as he liked to ride out to the small towns, bordering upon the city of Mexico, and take a dinner with the bonny lasses and countrymen, inhabiting those villages. He used to ask my friend to loan him his horse, to take these excursions just around the capital; and, as his requests were granted with so good a grace, he in a short time went so far as to ask the loan of this favorite animal, to go to Cuernavaca, a distance of eighteen leagues, or fifty miles. As this happened pretty often, our friend complained to me one day, at the indiscretion of the friar. I asked him if he could procure me a friar's dress, for a few days, and leave his horse with me, for the same time. He did so. I dressed myself in the friar's dress, and went in where the horse was. I took a good whip in my hand, and made him do penance for no other sin but that of too much gentleness. In going out I took off the friar's dress, and went in again in my own dress, and handled him gently. I repeated the operation a few days, at the end of which, I took the horse back to his master, and told him he might lend him to the friar whenever he pleased. A day or two after, he came to my store. Your remedy, said he, has had a marvellous effect. Our monk has just left my house, perfectly persuaded that my horse is possessed with the devil. For, when the holy personage came up to take him by the bridle to get on him, he was so frightened, and wheeled round so quick, and flew away from him with so much terror, that one would have said he took him for the destroying angel. The friar crossed himself many times, hurried away with all haste to his convent, to sprinkle himself abundantly with holy water, and never asked my friend for his horse again.

TO TEACH YOUR HORSE, SO THAT HE WILL LET NO ONE BUT YOURSELF COME NEAR HIM.

Whilst your horse is eating, let another person come in to him with a stick sharpened at the end. Let him prick his nose with it, to irritate him; but slightly, drawing back at the same time. Let him repeat the same an instant afterwards, and every time the horse begins to eat again. Come to him yourself, and caress him and talk to him. Go out again, and cause another person to come in with the sharpened stick; but not the same one that came in at first. Let him fret him in the same manner as the other did. Call him out and go in yourself; handle the horse gently, and talk to him. Call in a third, and a fourth, and perform the same; always retiring suddenly from the horse, as if they were afraid of him, every time he leers at them, or endeavors to bite them. These lessons, repeated a few days, will inspire your horse with so much mistrust against every person but yourself, and a certain confidence in his own strength, that he will not suffer any one but yourself to come near him.

TO PREVENT A HORSE FROM PULLING UPON HIS BRIDLE-REINS, IN ORDER TO BREAK THEM.

Put a halter, (of that kind which Spaniards call a jaquima, used to ride young horses: it goes over their ears, comes down and crosses their nose, and has a throat-latch to it,) upon your horse, so strong that it cannot be easily broken, and tie it to a tree so small that it will bend a little, if the horse pulls with all his strength. Scare him. Run up before him. Give him even a light stroke or two with the whip: speaking to him to be quiet, whenever he pulls upon the rope. In a short time, he will see that it is impossssible for him to break it; and, by exercising him twice a day for half an hour, each day in about a week, he will no longer pull upon the halter, when you scare him, and consequently will stand still afterwards, when hitched by the bridle.

THE MEXICAN MODE OF PREVENTING A HORSE FROM BREAKING HIS BRIDLE.

The Mexicans, when they ride out, always carry a beautiful hair rope, hanging from their horse's neck. Whenever they stop, they hitch or tie their horses by this rope; and this simple method keeps them from breaking their bridle-reins. I would advise every one to do the same; especially if he stops long, is on a journey, or rides a stud. Merchants and saddlers may, perhaps, not like this advice, but I write for all. They likewise sell ropes.

HOW TO MANAGE A HORSE THAT GETS THE STUDS, OR ONE THAT STOPS AND WILL NOT ADVANCE A STEP WHEN YOU PUT HIM TO A PLOUGH, &c.

When your horse is harnessed, and put before the plough, and you find it impossible to drive him forward, either by gentle or rough means, drive down a strong stake or post, at the very place where he stops. Let it be so strong that he cannot break it by pulling. Then put a rope upon him equally strong; tie him rather short. Take out your watch, if you have one; if not, look at the sun. Let him remain in this position for twelve hours, without eating or drinking. If the days are short, I would advise you to tie him a little before sun-set, and let him remain all night. Go to him, untie him, and then speak to him to go on. He will undoubtedly advance. Make him plough two or three rounds; then unharness him, and give him something to eat, after having watered him, and put him again in the plough, should he stop again, do with him as at first, and let him stand nine or ten hours. It is rare that you have to repeat the operation: almost all horses go after the first time they have been thus managed.

HOW TO TEACH A HORSE TO LIE DOWN AT THE WORD OF COMMAND.

Tie up the horse's right foot with a handkerchief, or a buckled strap, or something that is not so hard, as a common rope. Hold him close by the bridle-reins. Then take a small stick in your right hand, and strike gently upon the horse's left leg, pulling downwards at the same time upon the bridle-reins, which you hold in your left hand, speaking to the horse, and telling him to lie down. Every time you strike his left leg, bear a little against him, and pull upon the bridle, saying to him, "Lie down, sir!" The horse, after several repetitions of the strokes, tries to lift up his left leg; but, as the other is tied up, this motion naturally throws him upon his knees. Now push him gently, till he lies upon his side. After he has remained several minutes in this position, untie his left leg, and say, "Stand up!" After he gets up, pat him in the forehead and all over, and lead him about a little. By repeating these lessons a few times, the horse will lie down at the word of command, by your pulling a little upon the bridle-reins, and leaning against him. When I practice this upon a wild horse that I have just been breaking, it is surprising to see how quick he will learn to lie down. He will do it in less than one half the time which one that has been broken in the common way will be, in doing the same, and very often in one fourth.

HOW TO TEACH A HORSE TO COUNT ANY NUMBER.

Take the horse's left foot in your right hand; lift it up, and strike it upon the ground, counting one, at the same time. Strike again, and count two, and again, and count three, &c. to ten: when you pronounce this last number, raise your voice, so that it will be a little more audible than it was in the other numbers, and let the horse's foot fall at the same time. Now count fifteen, or any other number, in the same manner; always telling the horse to count ten, fifteen, &c., and pronouncing the number you tell in a more audible manner, letting his foot fall at the same time. In a few lessons, he will learn to count at the word of command, and will stop at any number, whenever you raise your voice a little. In the same manner, you may make him tell what o'clock it is, &c.

EASY MODE OF FATTENING A HORSE IN A SHORT TIME.

The first day you take a lean horse, and wish to put him in a situation, as quick as possible, to be able to perform a journey or any other fatigue: give him, in the morning, twelve ears of corn, soaked twenty four hours in clean water. Scatter half a spoonful of fine salt over it; then let him eat hay or fodder for one hour. At noon, give him eight ears more, and a little fodder. Let him stand till five o'clock, if the weather is warm, and then bathe him: feed him as in the morning, and give him hay, grass or fodder, not quite so much as he would eat, The second day, bleed him by one or two slight incisions in the mouth, and give him sixteen ears of corn in the morning, and what grass or fodder he will eat in half an hour, and no more than four ears of corn at noon. Feed him in the evening as in the morning, after having bathed him as before, and augment the quantity of fodder. If the weather is cool, curry him and rub him well, instead of bathing. Third day, give him as much corn as he will eat, and fodder at discretion all night. Feed him as above, at seven or eight o'clock in the morning, and give him no hay or fodder, and nothing at noon: continue in this manner, observing to scatter a little salt upon his corn every third day. It will be necessary, after the third or fourth day, to ride him a mile or two twice a day. A horse managed in this manner, will be fatter at the end of ten or twelve days, than one fed in the common way will be in a month.

A horse upon a journey, from September till April, requires no feeding, from the time you start in the morning till you stop at night. He will stand the journey better, and lose less flesh. I have travelled thousands of miles in the Mexican states, and have always found it to be the case, with the exception of those hot countries bordering on the Pacific Ocean, where I fed a little at noon—started a little early, and rode late, on account of the heat, which is equally great at all seasons of the year. A horse fed as I have directed for fifteen days, may then eat his corn without being soaked; and, though these directions are more particularly intended for this country, and for horses taken from the prairies, still, the directions will hold good in all countries and all climates: allowing something, however, for the different length of days in different seasons and climates. When on a journey, let a horse drink as often as he wishes.

A REMEDY FOR A HORSE THAT WILL NOT FATTEN, THOUGH WELL FED.

There are some horses that will not fatten, though you feed them with the greatest care; and, at the same time, they are perfectly healthy in other respects. Give to such a horse a pint of pretty strong decoction of the root of poke-weed. It generally causes him to sweat copiously, and it often happens, that one dose is sufficient to effect a radical cure; but, it may be necessary to repeat the dose two or three times: after which, treat him as you would a horse taken out of the prairie to be fattened according to the method laid down in this work.

TO PREVENT A HORSE'S BACK FROM GETTING SORE, EVEN ON A LONG JOURNEY.

The best method I ever found, to keep a horse's back from getting sore, on a long journey, is: in the first place, to procure a saddle, with a saddle-tree sufficiently open as not to come in contact with the spine. If it be a Spanish saddle, or one of the common saddles used in herding cattle in this country, add to it a couple of cushions filled with wool well picked and clean, considerably thicker at the upper part, where they come nighest to the spine, and thinner as they descend upon the ribs of the horse. Fine wool is far preferable to hair, or any other substance I ever made use of. Put under the saddle a small saddle-blanket, which should likewise be of wool. When you stop, even for a few minutes, unloose or slacken the girt, and

THE HORSE ABOUT TO FALL.

if you stop half an hour, take off your saddle: especially if the weather be warm. When you stop at night, curry your horse well, and bathe his back in cold water, if the weather be warm. Give him as much corn and fodder as he will eat, but always give him the fodder an hour, or at least half an hour before you give him the corn. Arise early in the morning, and go yourself, or send a servant of confidenc, to see that your horse eats as much as he will before you start on your journey; for good feeding is likewise a pretty good remedy to prevent a horse's back from getting sore, because a horse in good order is less liable to be hurt than a lean one. Should your horse get foundered on the road, ride him or make him walk for at least two hours: after which bleed him copiously in the mouth, and continue your journey the next day, without fear of his failing; for though he should still limp a little, he will be well by night. I had forgot to observe, that before you bleed him, you must rub all his legs well, and bathe them in cold water. In rubbing them, it must always be done by beginning at the upper part and rubbing downwards.

HOW TO TREAT A HORSE UPON A JOURNEY.

From September to March, never feed your horse at noon. It is good to start early in the morning. When you stop to eat breakfast, unloose your girt, and, if the weather be warm, take off the saddle. If you stop for dinner, do the same. Let your horse drink as often as he pleases; but give him nothing to eat, till you stop at night, or, rather, a little before sun-set. When you stop, it is good, if your horse is warm, to let him walk about a few minutes, before you take off the saddle. When he gets perfectly dry, have him curried; and, in very warm weather, bathe him. Give him fodder for an hour before you give him his corn, if you feed with corn; but if with oats or barley, you may give either to him at the same time that you give him his hay. When you start in the morning, go on rather moderately till ten or eleven o'clock. Then you may go a little faster, and increase your pace in the afternoon. When you stop at night, give your horse as much corn and fodder as he will eat. Let hay or fodder remain in the rack all night, but not the corn. Give him twenty or thirty ears, if he will eat so many, before you start. From April to the first of September, feed a little at noon. Clean the mud out of your horse's hoofs, every now and then; that is, every morning, or second morning; and, if you perceive that your horse often gets balls of hard, dry earth in them, rub soft soap upon the inside of them, and that will prevent the mud from sticking.

A HORSE THAT IS APT TO STUMBLE THROUGH CARELESSNESS.

Feed well: that, in the first place, will give him strength to stand upon his feet firmly, and be able to support his rider; and, should he still stumble, ride him with a Spanish bridle, and hold the reins rather short, and check him whenever he stumbles. This is, perhaps, the most efficacious remedy known. Some horses are so constructed that they are natural stumblers. It is very difficult to cure such a one of this defect, though by using him some time to the Spanish bit, he will stumble less.

HOW TO BREAK A MULE BY THE SECRET: AND THE DIFFERENCE THERE IS TO BE OBSERVED BETWEEN A MULE AND A HORSE.

A mule seems to belong to all three classes of horses, as to vices: it will run at a man, bite, and strike at him, like a horse of the first class; it will again fly from him, like one of the second class; and kick, and appear to be afraid of every thing, like a horse of the third class: and yet I have broken two or three in a day; and one day, I broke four in ten hours and a half, so that a man might handle their feet, and take them up with the greatest ease; saddle and bridle them, and put two or three boys upon them, and ride them through the streets of a populous town. This I did, in the city of Jalapa, seventy-five miles above the city of Vera Cruz, on the road to Mexico. But this may be looked upon as a rare case; for it generally takes from six to eight hours to break a mule, so as to ride him with safety. Now, a man may know how to break a horse, according to the rules I have here laid down, and completely fail in his first attempts upon a mule. In the first place, it is absolutely necessary to have a halter upon the mule, of that kind called a jaguima, in the Spanish language. Now, when I draw nigh them, as is indicated in the manner which I follow in coming up to a wild horse, for the first time, I always take up the rope, which is tied to the headstall of the halter, and then approach with much precaution, but without any signs of fear, &c., &c. Now, as I write for the timid, as well as for the courageous and intrepid, and as I look upon a mule as a most treacherous animal, I will here state, that all these precautions may be rendered unnecessary, by making a pen just big enough to put the mule in, and so high that it cannot jump over it; and let the bars be far enough apart to pass your hand between them and handle the mule. The pen must be made in such a manner that you can go around it on each side, as well behind as before, and be able to get upon it so as to saddle the mule, when you find it sufficiently gentle to proceed thus far. Then continue the operation as with a horse, but with this difference: you ought always to load the mule with bags of sand, or the like, and exercise it before you ride it. A weight of about two hundred pounds is not too much for the first time. As for any thing further, do as you would with a horse, &c.

The same pen you make for one mule, may serve for others which are of about the same size; and thus you may break, in a very few days, a great many mules, so as to go immediately to work with them, without laming them by blows and rough usage, which is often the cause of their being refractory the rest of their lives. I have broken a sufficient number of them to bear witness of the truth of this assertion. All those persons who may have learnt any part of my secret of breaking horses in a few hours, have remained perfectly silent with regard to mules, though they have undoubtedly tried their skill upon them, but in vain.

HOW THALES, ONE OF THE SEVEN WISE MEN OF GREECE, CORRECTED A MULE OF THE HABIT OF LYING DOWN EVERY TIME IT PASSED A CERTAIN RIVER.

THALES, one of the seven wise men of Greece, had a mule which used to carry loads of salt from one place to another, in consequence of which, it had to cross a very wide, but rather shallow river. It so happened one day, that whilst it was crossing the river, being heavily loaded, it stumbled and fell down, and remained some time in the middle of the water, which soon melted and washed away the salt that was in the bags. The animal, finding itself thus alleviated and discharged of its load, was able to jump up and pursue its journey without fatigue: from thence it concluded that the said fall and immersion in the river had been favorable and beneficial to it; therefore, when it had to cross the river a second time with a load of salt, it stopped in the midst of the river, and plunged in such a manner that its load soon melted away; and this happened every time it passed the stream; nor was it possible to break it of this trick, either by words or blows, though vigorously and well-applied, At last, the wise Thales bethought himself of this stratagem: He loaded the beast with a very bulky load of sponge; the mule, according to custom, plunged into the water, and remained some time; but, when it got up, it could hardly stagger under the weight of its load, and, instead of relief, found itself oppressed to such a degree, that it ever after crossed the river with the greatest care, so as not to fall in the water and increase the weight of its load.

HOW TO MAKE A DULL HORSE APPEAR METTLESOME AND FULL OF FIRE FOR A SHORT TIME.

Take of red pepper, of the strongest kind, a small handful. Pound it fine, and add half a spoonful of vinegar to it. Put the whole into a small bag, made of linen, and tie it to that part of the crupper which goes immediately under the horse's tail. Buckle the crupper rather short, so that it will press upon the little bag, as the horse trots off. The juice will flow out of the bag, and come in contact with a certain part, which will immediately have the most wonderful effect upon the horse imaginable. He will champ his bit, if you hold him in, and appear to be all fire and mettle. When you ride off, he will hold up his head, stick his ears forward, lift his feet with agility, and caper about like a young colt. In a word, he will act the part of a fiery, mettlesome horse, full of vigor and spiritedness.

THAT PART, OR THOSE PARTS OF THE MEXICAN STATES IN WHICH THE BEST RACE OF HORSES IS TO BE FOUND, AND SOME OF THEIR QUALITIES.

The horses that are brought to Louisiana, under the name of Spanish horses, generally come from Caahuila, Tamaulipas, and Neuvo Leon. They are of a pretty good size, and commonly of a vicious disposition. They are very much affected by the change of climate. They are likewise used to a better kind of grass than that growing in Louisiana. They are much larger than the creole horses, and when acclimated live longer. When mixed with the creole horses, they form a good race, far better than the creole horses. Planters generally suffer great loss in purchasing northern horses, which are so much affected by the climate that hundreds of them die every year. A better and more serviceable race of horses may be raised, by procuring northern mares, and putting them with creole studs. They will not only stand the climate as well as the creole horses, but will render more service than the northern horses, and do not require half so much care. But a race of horses, far superior to either of the above-mentioned, can be raised, by procuring some of those beautiful Andalusian studs, and putting them with northern mares. This would be really improving the race of horses in this country. I would likewise advise the planters to procure both mares and horses, and raise at least some elegant riding horses from this Andalusian race. I have more than once mounted upon a fiery Arabian steed, that hardly seemed to touch the ground, as he bounded over the plains—I have likewise ridden upon some of the finest horses raised in New Spain—and, for my life, I have found it difficult to distinguish the difference between the former and the latter. They are of the same size—their shape is the same—their long, floating mane the same—their beautiful, small and well turned hoof the same, and so hard that they travel over vastly high and rocky mountains, without being shod. Add to this, their hardiness to undergo fatigue. I have ridden one of these horses for twenty days together, going from fifty to fifty-five miles a day, and frequently changing from a cold to a hot climate, and vice versa; for in New Spain, climates are hot or cold, according as they are higher or lower; and this I have done, without my horse ever appearing in the least jaded, or the leaner for it. The rider himself feels much more at his ease, than he does when riding a heavy, clumsy horse, that moves along like a camel, and is remarkable only on account of his unwieldliness, and is, as a Kentuckian would say, "waste timber!" Besides, the Andalusian or Arabian breed are the most elegant easy-going horses in the world. They have no resemblance to those Spanish horses which are brought to this country.

Now, as I have mentioned some of their qualities, I will inform the amateur where he can best procure them. In going by land to the Mexican states, the first horses of this kind to be met with, are raised upon the Hacienda del Xaral, (pronounced Haral, and often written with a J, Jaral,) two hundred and sixty miles this side of the city of San Louis Potosi, in the state of the same name. Still further on, in the states of Guanajuato and Quenetaro, the same race of horses is to be found, and likewise in other places: but, those I here mention, would be by far the most convenient places to procure them, as they are not so far distant as others from Tampico, should one wish to bring them by sea to New Orleans, nor so far from this state, should one prefer bringing them by land. All of these fine horses, I here mention, are raised upon the table-lands, where excessive heat is never felt: and yet, if you take them down to the hot countries upon the coast, they will, even there, do double the service of one of the hot-country horses, in their own climate. I speak from experience, for I have tried both. They likewise possess another good quality, which is that of being the most sure-footed animals in the world, of the horse kind; not even excepting a mule.

CAUTION TO BE OBSERVED, IN CUTTING OR PARING THE HOOFS OF YOUR HORSES IN THIS COUNTRY, WHERE HORSES GENERALLY GO UNSHOD.

When you cut or pare the hoofs of your horses, be careful to cut them so as not to let that soft part, which is in the middle of the foot, commonly called the frog, rise above the outside of the hoof; for if you do, it will undoubtedly make the horse limp. When it is too big, it must be cut off. Nobody will do it so efficaciously as a blacksmith, and it is better to pay such a one some trifle than to lame your horse.

CAUTION TO THOSE WHO RAISE HORSES OR MULES.

He that would raise a good stock of horses or mules, must have good pasture-ground, and take special care that the colts do not want for food in the winter time, and more particularly the first two years. More depends upon the first two years, than any thing that can be done afterwards; for a colt that is badly fed, and allowed to suffer hunger and cold while he is young, will rarely or never make a large horse; whereas, if he has been well fed for two years, he is more able to support hardship afterwards, though I by no means advise any one to neglect him at any time.

TO ACCUSTOM A HORSE TO STAY IN A PLACE.

If you buy a horse in one part of the country, and take him to another, and the horse returns of his own accord to his former abode, cause another person, (if the person be his old master, so much the better,) to take your horse and tie him up, and whip him severely, and let him stand all night without eating any thing whatever. In the morning, let the same person come again to the horse, and give him another good discipline: immediately afterwards, go to your horse, mount him, and ride him back to the place where you wish him to stay, and give him some salt, and plenty to eat. Keep him inclosed for two days, well fed, handled and caressed. Then cause him to be taken to his first place of residence. Let any person catch him, tie him up, and whip him, as at first, leaving him tied all night, without eating. Go to him, get upon him, and ride him home; caress and feed him well, and give him a little salt. Let him loose, at the end of two days, upon trial; if he does not return at the end of four days, have him caught, caressed and fed, and salt given to him, and then let loose. But should he return a third time, which would be a rare case, repeat the discipline. I seldom or never knew this remedy to fail.

TO MAKE A GENTLE HORSE, NOT USED TO A CARRIAGE GO IN IT.

Harness your horse: handle him in the forehead a few minutes. Let some one lead him, whilst you hold the reins and go behind him with a whip in your hand. Make him advance, by speaking to him; then speak to him to stop, at the same time you pull upon the reins. Exercise him a few minutes in this way, then handle him again in the forehead. Make him advance: let the person who led him now go before, at a little distance, then further off, till at last the horse will suffer himself to be driven, without any one being before him. Now let him drag a small piece of wood, with some one going before as at first, till he suffers himself to be driven without. Exercise him a few minutes, in this way, then with something larger, that will make considerable noise. I have always made use of a barrel, fixed so that it would roll round, and in which I put a quantity of round stones; but, as stones are difficult to be procured in this part of the country, their place can be supplied by something else. Give the horse a good exercise, in the same gentle, progressive manner as above, till he will suffer himself to be driven with this last load in every direction, without the necessity of any one going before him. Then put him to an empty cart, and continue on, in the same progressive manner. Never pull upon the reins, to stop your horse, without speaking to him. I have never yet failed of success in putting a horse to a coach or gig; but, it is certain, that there are some horses so fiery and vicious, that few persons would have patience enough to succeed. I here speak of those horses that have contracted vicious habits, after having been broken for a long time. Never fail to give your horse a very small quantity of salt, after having exercised him to go in a cart or gig. Do not give him more than a thimble-full at a time. He will generally go well the first day; but he ought to have a few hours exercise each day, for a few days.

A HORSE THAT STOPS, AND REFUSES TO GO, WHEN IN A CARRIAGE.

If a horse stops, and refuses to go, or runs back, go up before him, handle him in the forehead and coax him. If he is not an old offender, he will go off in about fifteen minutes. If he has been spoiled for a long time, it requires more patience to correct him.

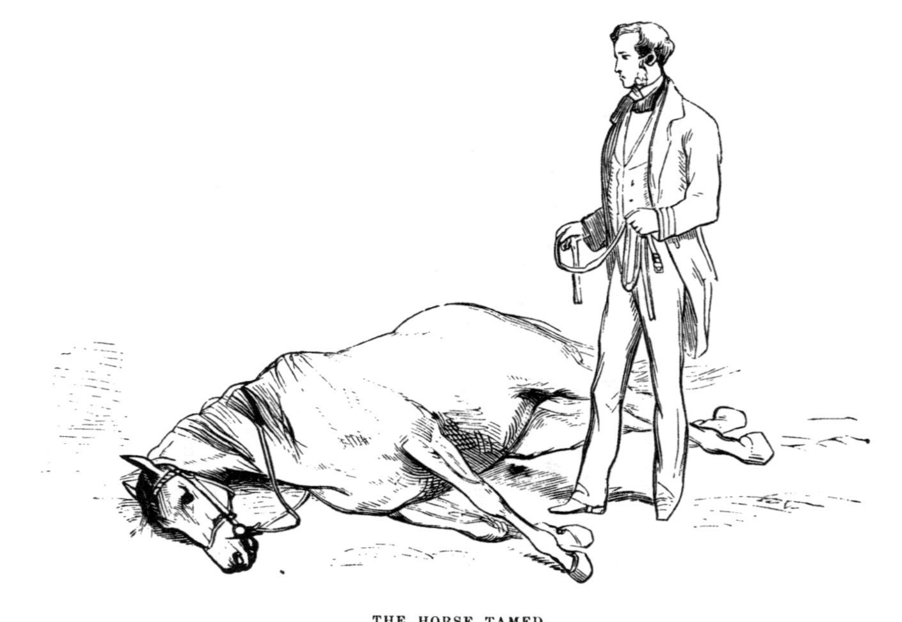

THE HORSE TAMED.

A MODE OF BREAKING WILD HORSES, VERY DIFFERENT FROM THAT DISCOVERED BY ME.

I have seen a wild horse taken and shut up in a stable. The man who was to gentle or tame him, took a whip, such as a coachman uses, and went in to him; and, as the horse was frightened, and ran away from him, he fell to whipping him most unmercifully. At the end of half an hour, the horse, seeing it impossible to escape the whip by running away, advanced towards the man who had been his persecutor. The man threw down his whip, and began to handle him; but the horse, at the end of a few minutes, began to be refractory, when he took it up again, and repeated the lesson with so much severity, that the horse soon came back to him. This he continued for some time; when, at the end of about two hours, he saddled the horse and drove him about with his whip, making him come up to him every now and then, till at last he mounted him and rode off very well. I observed, that the horse frequently trembled, when he went to get on him, notwithstanding he rode him off pretty well; he appeared to be afraid of many objects he met with, and was far, very far from being that gentle, docile animal, tamed by the simple, natural means made use of in my method of breaking horses. Besides this, those horses do not remain gentle. I speak from experience.

ANOTHER MODE OF BREAKING A HORSE FOR A FEW HOURS.

Stop up the horse's ears, so that he cannot hear at all, and you can very soon handle him as if he were a gentle horse; but, when you unstop his ears, he will become as wild as ever. If you perform this two or three times upon the same horse, it will have no effect upon him at last.

ADVICE TO FARMERS, CONCERNING THE GENTLING OF YOUNG COWS.

Though I did not intend to say any thing about horned cattle, it may not, perhaps, be amiss to relate what I have experienced and been eye-witness to, in the state of Louisiana, concerning the gentling of young cows, since I discovered the secret of breaking horses in a few hours. Whenever I have had a heifer or young cow to gentle, (it must be observed, that they are much wilder here than in the northern states,) I have made it a practice to have them tied by the horns to a post, and have made a servant begin to handle them well all over, speaking to them uninterruptedly; and this he did for two or three mornings, before milking them, always finishing by giving them a little salt. At the end of three or four days, they never failed of becoming gentle, and could be milked without being tied. Though I have seen by experience, that horned cattle, especially bulls, are much less sensible to the touch than horses, a part of which may possibly be owing to the thickness of their skin, yet even with them I have done much. Let any one who will, do more.

THE ASTONISHING MANNER IN WHICH I TAMED OR GENTLED A WILD DEER.

The second day after my arrival in the town of Tantoyuca, I presented myself to the first Alcade, or chief magistrate of the town. I showed him the documents I had brought with me from the President and other authorities, and expressed a desire of putting in practice, in that town the ability I possessed of taming, in a few hours, wild horses. The Alcade seemed to be of a morose, surly temper, and answered me, saying, he did not believe in witches, nor miracles, and though he said he respected the President's document, yet he believed he had been imposed upon, &c. He appeared not even disposed to give me a trial. He had a brother-in-law, a Spaniard, a genteel, wealthy gentleman: this man was very much disposed to favor my undertaking. He possessed numerous herds of wild horses. He gave me one of his houses to live in, whilst I staid in the town, for I had my wife and family with me. About six o'clock, (this was in Febuary, 1826,) whilst we were all sitting at the door, taking the air, a wild deer came bouncing by us. It had been chased out of the woods by a leopard or a tiger. The large spotted tiger and leopard are both natives of this country, and are often seen within half a mile of the towns in the Guanteca. The deer ran down opposite the Alcade's house: there, a man threw a rope upon it, and caught it. I immediately went to the man, bought the deer, and told him to tie it and bring it up to my house. He accordingly did so. I untied it, and shut it up in a room, where it remained all night. The next morning, before sun-rise, I went to it, and began the operation of gentling; and, at nine o'clock, I made it follow me to the Alcade's, accompanied by his brother-in-law. The Alcade was so delighted at seeing the deer follow me into his house, that he gave me every facility to perform in that town, which I did, and brought away a fine purse of doubloons, which he and his friends gave me, as a gratification for having broken a wild horse in their presence.

This deer having been shut up all night, as I have observed, I got up early in the morning, and went to the room in which it was confined. As I opened the door, it appeared almost frightened to death. I shut the door, however, and remained perfectly still for some time. The deer had retired to the further corner of the room, which was very small: it had turned round, and was looking at me. I kept my position, with my left hand stretched out, for half an hour before I began to move, as slow as possible, towards the deer, which kept its eyes fixed steadfast upon me, and never stirred, till I got nigh enough to touch it. I moved my hand for some time, before I dared to let it fall upon its head: at last, I ventured to let the end of my fingers fall, as lightly as possible, upon its head; it trembled and flinched a little; I repeated, with the greatest rapidity, those very light touches, and in less than five minutes, as I suppose, (for it was impossible for me to look at my watch without frightening the deer,) I began to rub it upon the head; and, in less than half an hour, I took its head under my arm, and handled it all over in two hours from the time I went in to it. I made my servant and several others go to it, and stroke and rub it. It was a full-grown deer, and not less than two or three years old. The mode of taming it consisted in stroking it gently, and taking its head in my arms, &c. I relate this circumstance more to prove the astonishing effect the tact has upon some animals, and to point out the different ways of applying it, than from any benefit resulting from taming this latter kind of animals.

A REMEDY FOR AN OX THAT LIES DOWN, AND WONT GET UP.

I have seen some oxen lie down, when put before the plough, and show so much obstinacy, that they suffered themselves to be whipped most unmercifully, and even burnt, without showing signs of obedience. If an ox lies down and will not get up, either by gentle or rough means, tie him in such a manner that it will be impossible for him to get up. Let him remain in this situation, without eating or drinking, for ten hours: then untie him, and he will not fail to go off. Let him go two or three rounds, and then feed him well. It is not common for him to return to his former offence, unless he has been an old offender; in which case, let him remain tied two or three hours longer, and he will not fail of leaving off his old tricks.

A CURIOUS METHOD OF TEACHING TURKIES TO DANCE AT THE SOUND OF THE TRIANGLE OR ANY OTHER MUSICAL INSTRUMENT.

It is a well known fact, that in the East Indies, camels are often taught to dance at the sound of music. I knew that this was done by putting them upon hot floors, &c. They are afterwards exhibited at public spectacles. I never had learned the precise course pursued; yet notwithstanding, I undertook to teach a dog to dance. I heated large pieces of tin plate, put the dog upon them, and at the same time struck upon a triangle, that being the easiest instrument I knew of. I tried this several times, without any other success than having most miserably burnt two or three dogs' feet in the experiments. At last, in one of my chemical operations, (for I was then teaching chemistry to a few young gentleman,) I made use of the sand-bath. It immediately occurred to me, that in teaching an animal to dance by means of heat, the heat ought to be tempered by something similar to the sand-bath. I therefore determined to make a new trial; and, having no dog at hand, I made choice of four good-looking turkies, two males and two females. I made two cages; the bottom of one was made of tin plates, upon which I strewed a certain portion of fine sand. Then I put fire under the cage. The turkies were in the other cage, which had a door of communication with the one having a tin bottom. When I thought the bottom of the cage sufficiently hot, I drove the turkies from the one to the other, shut the door, and began to strike rapidly and loudly upon the triangle, which I held in my hand. The sensation of heat which the turkies experienced, caused them to skip about as if they had been possessed with some evil spirit. After letting them continue their exercise for a quarter of an hour or so, I opened the door and drove them back into the first cage, and at the same time stopped playing. Then I fed them well, and lastly turned them loose in the yard. The next day, I made them go through the same ceremony, before I gave them any thing to eat, and so on, for a quarter of an hour or more every day, for ten days; at the end of which, I struck upon the triangle before I turned them into the hot cage. Only one of them, more docile than the other three, began to jump about a little. The others, it is true, looked up, and seemed, as it were, astonished. I was then fully convinced that they would all shortly learn to dance, if I continued the same method of giving them lessons. I accordingly continued on, in the same manner, for twenty days more; at the end of which, I let them loose one day in a room, and began to strike violently upon the triangle. All four of the turkies began to skip and run about, keeping pretty close to one another, and changing every minute their position. It was the most ludicrous, and, at the same time, entertaining sight imaginable. The impression which the sound of the triangle had made upon them, on account of their having felt the heat at the bottom of the cage, every time they had heard that music, became a lasting one; and they would begin to dance, ever after, though in the yard amidst the other turkies, whenever they heard the sound of that instrument. They generally separated themselves from the others, and run together. They may be taught with any other instrument, as well as with the triangle. It will take much longer to teach a dog, than a turkey. The reason is, as I suppose, that the dog is not so easily deceived. The only difficulty attending this mode of teaching turkies to dance is, to keep your tin plates neither too hot nor too cold; for, if too hot, they will get their feet burnt; and, if too cold, they won't dance. I sold the four above-mentioned turkies, for four doubloons, to a man who went about exhibiting various curiosities.

REMEDY FOR THE GRIPES, OR COLIC.

Give to the horse a pint of port or claret wine, with a small nutmeg grated fine, and half a spoonful of powdered ginger, all well mixed, and given rather hotter than lukewarm. The best method is to get ready some boiling hot water, then put the nutmeg and ginger, together with a little loaf sugar, into a vessel, and pour the hot water upon them, and cover it for three minutes; then add the wine, and give this dose to the horse pretty warm. It generally gives relief in a short time. My intention is not to say any thing upon farriery, except two or three of the most common diseases to which horses are subject. Much has already been written by able professors.

CONCERNING THE BOTS.

In twenty-seven years time, I never had a horse die of the bots. I believe that almost every body is convinced that the bots come from the eggs or knits, which are deposited upon the horse's hair, by that troublesome fly, resembling a bee in color. This has always been my opinion. Now, as it is generally known, that a horse that has the bots, does not appear to suffer, till he is too far gone to be cured, to prevent the fatal effects of this disease, I have made it a practice to give my horses, in the month of September, the following remedy: Of olive oil, honey and lemon-juice, each, two ounces and a half: mix and give these to the horse; the next day purge well. Whether a horse be inclined or not to have the bots, this remedy will do him no hurt.

THE BLIND STAGGERS.

It is believed, that the disease called STAGGERS, is generally occasioned by a diseased state of the stomach. Copious and timely bleeding is the sheet-anchor on which we must depend. I shall, however, give the following recipe, which has often proved serviceable: Take of oil of peppermint, one scruple; tincture of valerian, one ounce; assafœtida, five drachms: mix for a dose.

TAMING OF WILD HORSES.

By J. S. RAREY,

THE AMERICAN HORSE TAMER.

THE THREE FUNDAMENTAL PRINCIPLES OF MY THEORY;

Founded on the Leading Characteristics of the Horse.

First.—That he is so constituted by nature that he will not offer resistance to any demand made of him which he fully comprehends, if made in a way consistent with the laws of his nature.

Second.—That he has no consciousness of his strength beyond his experience, and can be handled according to our will without force.

Third.—That we can, in compliance with the laws of his nature by which he examines all things new to him, take any object, however frightful around, over, or on him, that does not inflict pain, without causing him to fear.

To take these assertions in order, I will first give you some of the reasons why I think he is naturally obedient, and will not offer resistance to anything fully comprehended. The horse, though possessed of some faculties superior to man's, being deficient in reasoning powers, has no knowledge of right or wrong, of free will and independent government, and knows not of any imposition practised upon him, however unreasonable these impositions may be. Consequently, he cannot come to any decision as to what he should or should not do, because he has not the reasoning faculties of man to argue the justice of the thing demanded of him. If he had, taking into consideration his superior strength, he would be useless to man as a servant. Give him mind in proportion to his strength, and he will demand of us the green fields for his inheritance, where he will roam at leisure, denying the right of servitude at all. God has wisely formed his nature so that it can be operated upon by the knowledge of man according to the dictates of his will; and he might well be termed an unconscious, submissive servant. This truth we can see verified in every day's experience by the abuses practised upon him. Any one who chooses to be so cruel, can mount the noble steed and run him till he drops with fatigue, or, as is often the case with the more spirited, falls dead beneath his rider. If he had the power to reason, would he not rear and pitch his rider, rather than suffer him to run him to death? Or would he condescend to carry at all the vain impostor, who, with but equal intellect, was trying to impose on his equal rights and equally independent spirit. But happily for us, he has no consciousness of imposition, no thought of disobedience except by impulse caused by the violation of the law of his nature. Consequently, when disobedient, it is the fault of man.

Then, we can but come to the conclusion that, if a horse is not taken in a way at variance with the laws of his nature, he will do anything that he fully comprehends, without making any offer of resistance.

Second—The fact of the horse being unconscious of the amount of his strength can be proven to the satisfaction of any one. For instance, such remarks as these are common, and perhaps familiar to your recollection. One person says to another, "If that wild horse there was conscious of the amount of his strength, his owner would have no business with him in that vehicle; such light reins and harness too—if he knew he could snap them asunder in a minute and be as free as the air we breathe;" and, "That horse yonder, that is pawing and fretting to follow the company that is fast leaving him—if he knew his strength, he would not remain long fastened to that hitching post so much against his will, by a strap that would no more resist his powerful weight and strength than a cotton thread would bind a strong man." Yet these facts, made common by every-day occurrence, are not thought of as anything wonderful. Like the ignorant man who looks at the different phases of the moon, you look at these things as he looks at her different changes without troubling your mind with the question, "Why are these things so?" What would be the condition of the world if all our minds lay dormant? If men did not think, reason, and act, our undisturbed, slumbering intellects would not excel the imbecility of the brute; we should live in chaos, hardly aware of our existence. And yet, with all our activity of mind, we daily pass by unobserved that which would be wonderful if philosophized and reasoned upon; and with the same inconsistency wonder at that which a little consideration, reason, and philosophy would make but a simple affair.

Third—He will allow any object, however frightful in appearance, to come around, over, or on him, that does not inflict pain.

We know from a natural course of reasoning, that there has never been an effect without a cause, and we infer from this, that there can be no action

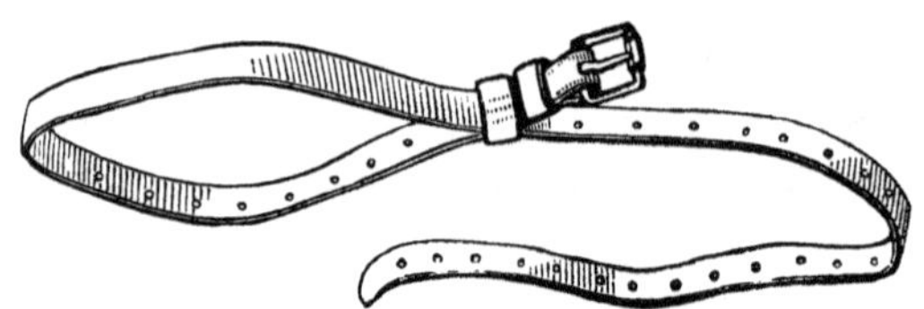

LEG STRAP.

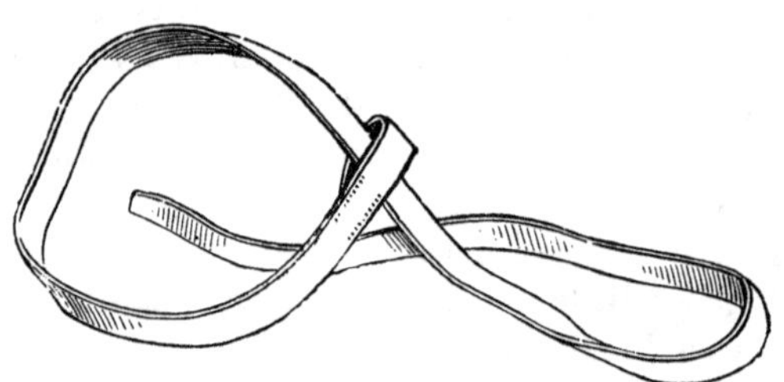

MR. RAREY'S EXTRA STRAP.

either in animate or inanimate matter, without there first being some cause to produce it. And from this self-evident fact we know that there is some cause for every impulse or movement of either mind or matter, and that this law governs every action or movement of the animal kingdom. Then, according to this theory, there must be some cause before fear can exist; and, if fear exists from the effect of imagination, and not from the infliction of real pain, it can be removed by complying with those laws of nature by which the horse examines an object, and determines upon its innocence or harm.

A log or stump by the road side may be, in the imagination of the horse, some great beast about to pounce upon him; but after you take him up to it and let him stand by it a little while, and touch it with his nose, and go through his process of examination, he will not care anything more about it. And the same principle and process will have the same effect with any other object, however frightful in appearance, in which there is no harm. Take a boy that has been frightened by a false face, or any other object that he could not comprehend at once; but let him take that face, or object in his hands and examine it, and he will not care anything more about it. This is a demonstration of the same principle.

With this introduction to the principles of my theory, I shall next attempt to teach you how to put it into practice; and, whatever instructions may follow you can rely on, as having been proven practically by my own experiments. And knowing from experience just what obstacles I have met with in handling bad horses, I shall try to anticipate them for you, and assist you in surmounting them, by commencing with the first steps to be taken with the colt, and accompany you through the whole task of breaking.

HOW TO SUCCEED IN GETTING THE COLT FROM PASTURE.

Go to the pasture and walk around the whole herd quietly, and at such a distance as not to cause them to scare and run. Then approach them very slowly, and if they stick up their heads and seem to be frightened, wait until they become quiet, so as not to make them run before you are close enough to drive them in the direction you want them to go. And when you begin to drive, do not flourish your arms or halloo, but gently follow them off, leaving the direction free for them that you wish them to take. Thus taking advantage of their ignorance, you will be able to get them into the pound as easily as the hunter drives the quails into his net. For, if they have always run in the pasture uncared for (as many horses do in prairie countries and on large plantations), there is no reason why they should not be as wild as the sportsman's birds, and require the same gentle treatment, if you want to get them without trouble; for the horse in his natural state, is as wild as any of the undomesticated animals, though more easily tamed than the most of them.

HOW TO STABLE A COLT WITHOUT TROUBLE.

The next step will be, to get the horse into a stable or shed. This should be done as quietly as possible, so as not to excite any suspicion in the horse of any danger befalling him. The best way to do this, is to lead a gentle horse into the stable first, and hitch him, then quietly walk around the colt and let him go in of his own accord. It is almost impossible to get men who have never practised on this principle to go slowly and considerately enough about it. They do not know that in handling a wild horse, above all other things, is that good old adage true, that "haste makes waste;" that is, waste of time—for the gain of trouble and perplexity.

One wrong move may frighten your horse, and make him think it necessary to escape at all hazards for the safety of his life—and thus make two hours' work of a ten minutes' job; and this would be all your own fault, and entirely unnecessary—for he will not run unless you run after him, and that would not be good policy unless you knew that you could outrun him, for you will have to let him stop of his own accord after all. But he will not try to break away unless you attempt to force him into measures. If he does not see the way at once, and is a little fretful about going in, do not undertake to drive him, but give him a little less room outside, by gently closing in around him. Do not raise your arms, but let them hang at your side, for you might as well raise a club: the horse has never studied anatomy, and does not know but that they will unhinge themselves and fly at him. If he attempts to turn back, walk before him, but do not run; and if he gets past you, encircle him again in the same quiet manner, and he.will soon find that you are not going to hurt him; and then you can walk so close around him that he will go into the stable for more room, and to get farther from you. As soon as he is in, remove the quiet horse and shut the door. This will be his first notion of confinement—not knowing how he got into such a place, nor how to get out of it. That he may take it as quietly as possible, see that the shed is entirely free from dogs, chickens, or anything that would annoy him. Then give him a few ears of corn, and let him remain alone fifteen or twenty minutes, until he has examined his apartment, and has become reconciled to his confinement.

TIME TO REFLECT.

And now, while your horse is eating those few ears of corn, is the proper time to see that your halter is ready and all right, and to reflect on the best mode of operations; for in horsebreaking it is highly important that you should be governed by some system. And you should know, before you attempt to do anything, just what you are going to do, and how you are going to do it. And, if you are experienced in the art of taming wild horses, you ought to be able to tell, within a few minutes, the length of time it would take you to halter the colt, and teach him to lead.

THE KIND OF HALTER.

Always use a leather halter, and be sure to have it made so that it will not draw tight around his nose if he pulls on it. It should be of the right size to fit his head easily and nicely; so that the nose-band will not be too tight or too low. Never put a rope halter on an unbroken colt, under any circumstances whatever. They have caused more horses to hurt or kill themselves than would pay for twice the cost of all the leather halters that have ever been needed for the purpose of haltering colts. It is almost impossible to break a colt that is very wild with a rope halter, without having him pull, rear, and throw himself, and thus endanger his life; and I will tell you why. It is just as natural for a horse to try to get his head out of anything that hurts it, or feels unpleasant, as it would be for you to try to get your hand out of a fire. The cords of the rope are hard and cutting; this makes him raise his head and draw on it, and as soon as he pulls, the slip noose (the way rope halters are always made) tightens, and pinches his nose, and then he will struggle for life, until, perchance, he throws himself; and who would have his horse throw himself, and run the risk of breaking his neck, rather than pay the price of a leather halter? But this is not the worst. A horse that has once pulled on his halter can never be as well broken as one that has never pulled at all.

REMARKS ON THE HORSE.

But before we attempt to do anything more with the colt, I will give you some of the characteristics of his nature, that you may better understand his motions. Every one that has ever paid any attention to the horse, has noticed his natural inclination to smell everything which to him looks new and frightful. This is their strange mode of examining everything. And, when they are frightened at anything, though they look at it sharply, they seem to have no confidence in this optical examination alone, but must touch it with the nose before they are entirely satisfied; and, as soon as this is done, all is right.

EXPERIMENT WITH THE ROBE.

If you want to satisfy yourself of this characteristic of the horse, and to learn something of importance concerning the peculiarities of his nature, &c., turn him into the barn-yard, or a large stable will do, and then gather up something that you know will frighten him—a red blanket, buffalo-robe, or something of that kind. Hold it up so that he can see it, he will stick up his head and snort. Then throw it down somewhere in the centre of the lot or barn, and walk off to one side. Watch his motions, and study his nature. If he is frightened at the object, he will not rest until he has touched it with his nose. You will see him begin to walk around the robe and snort, all the time getting a little closer, as if drawn up by some magic spell, until he finally gets within reach of it.

He will then very cautiously stretch out his neck as far as he can reach, merely touching it with his nose, as though he thought it was ready to fly at him. But after he has repeated these touches a few times, for the first time (though he has been looking at it all the while,) he seems to have an idea what it is. But now he has found, by the sense of feeling, that it is nothing that will do him any harm, and he is ready to play with it. And if you watch him closely, you will see him take hold of it with his teeth, and raise it up and pull at it. And in a few minutes you can see that he has not that same wild look about his eye, but stands like a horse biting at some familiar stump.

Yet the horse is never so well satisfied when he is about anything that has frightened him, as when he is standing with his nose to it. And, in nine cases out of ten, you will see some of that same wild look about him again, as he turns to walk from it. And you will probably see him looking back very suspiciously as he walks away, as though he thought it might come after him yet. And in all probability, he will have to go back and make another examination before he is satisfied. But he will familiarize himself with it, and, if he should run in that lot a few days, the robe that frightened him so much at first will be no more to him than a familiar stump.

SUGGESTIONS ON THE HABIT OF SMELLING.

We might very naturally suppose from the fact of the horse's applying his nose to everything new to him, that he always does so for the purpose of smelling these objects; but I believe that it is as much or more for the purpose of feeling, and that he makes use of his nose, or muzzle, (as it is sometimes called), as we would of our hands; because it is the only organ by which he can touch or feel anything with much susceptibility.

I believe that he invariably makes use of the four senses—seeing, hearing, smelling, and feeling—in all of his examinations, of which the sense of feeling is, perhaps, the most important. And I think that, in the experiment with the robe, his gradual approach and final touch with his nose was as much for the purpose of feeling as anything else, his sense of smell being so keen that it would not be necessary for him to touch his nose against anything in order to get the proper scent; for it is said that a horse can smell a man at the distance of a mile. And if the scent of the robe was all that was necessary, he could get that several rods off. But we know from experience, that if a horse sees and smells a robe a short distance from him, he is very much frightened (unless he is used to it) until he touches or feels it with his nose; which is a positive proof that feeling is the controlling sense in this case.

PREVAILING OPINION OF HORSEMEN.

It is a prevailing opinion among horsemen generally that the sense of smell is the governing sense of the horse. And Faucher, as well as others, has with that view got up receipts of strong smelling oils, &c., to tame the horse, sometimes using the chestnut of his leg, which they dry, grind into powder, and blow into his nostrils, sometimes using the oils of rhodium, origanum, &c., that are noted for their strong smell; and sometimes they scent the hand with the sweat from under the arm, or blow their breath into his nostrils, &c., &c. All of which, as far as the scent goes, have no effect whatever in gentling the horse, or conveying any idea to his mind; though the acts that accompany these efforts—handling him, touching him about the nose and head, and patting him, as they direct you should, after administering the articles, may have a very great effect, which they mistake to be the effect of the ingredients used. And Faucher, in his work, entitled "The Arabian Art of Taming

Horses," page 17, tells us how to accustom a horse to a robe, by administering certain articles to his nose; and goes on to say that these articles must first be applied to the horse's nose before you attempt to break him, in order to operate successfully.

Now, reader, can you, or any one else, give one single reason how scent can convey any idea to the horse's mind of what we want him to do? If not, then of course strong scents of any kind are of no avail in taming the unbroken horse. For, everything that we get him to do of his own accord, without force, must be accomplished by some means of conveying our ideas to his mind. I say to my horse, "Go-'long!" and he goes. "Ho!" and he stops; because these two words, of which he has learned the meaning by the tap of the whip and the pull of the rein that first accompanied them, convey the two ideas to his mind of go and stop.

Neither Faucher, nor any one else, can ever teach the horse a single thing by the means of scent alone.

How long do you suppose a horse would have to stand and smell a bottle of oil before he would learn to bend his knee and make a bow at your bidding, "Go yonder and bring your hat," or "Come here and lie down"? Thus you see the absurdity of trying to break or tame the horse by the means of receipts for articles to smell at, or medicine to give him, of any kind whatever.

The only science that has ever existed in the world, relative to the breaking of horses, that has been of any value, is that true method which takes them in their native state, and improves their intelligence.

POWEL'S SYSTEM OF APPROACHING THE COLT.

But, before we go further, I will give you Willis J. Powel's system of approaching a wild colt, as given by him in a work on the "Art of Taming Wild Horses." He says, "A horse is gentled by my secret in from two to sixteen hours." The time I have most commonly employed has been from four to six hours. He goes on to say, (see page 35, of this work).

REMARKS ON POWEL'S TREATMENT.—HOW TO GOVERN HORSES OF ANY KIND.

These instructions are very good, but not quite sufficient for horses of all kinds, and for haltering and leading the colt; but I have inserted them here because they give some of the true philosophy of approaching the horse, and of establishing confidence between man and horse. He speaks only of the kind that fear man.

To those who understand the philosophy of horsemanship, these are the easiest trained; for when we have a horse that is wild and lively, we can train him to our will in a very short time—for they are generally quick to learn, and always ready to obey. But there is another kind that are of a stubborn or vicious disposition; and although they are not wild, and do not require taming in the sense it is generally understood, they are just as ignorant as a wild horse, if not more so, and need to be taught just as much: and in order to have them obey quickly, it is very necessary that they should be made to fear their master; for, in order to obtain perfect obedience from any horse, we must first have him fear us, for our motto is, fear, love, and obey; and we must have the fulfilment of the first two before we can expect the latter; for it is by our philosophy of creating fear, love, and confidence, that we govern to our will every kind of horse whatever.

Then, in order to take horses as we find them, of all kinds, and to train them to our liking, we will always take with us, when we go into a stable to train a colt, a long switch whip (whalebone buggy-whips are the best), with a good silk cracker, so as to cut keenly and make a sharp report, which, if handled with dexterity, and rightly applied, accompanied with a sharp fierce word, will be sufficient to enliven the spirits of any horse. With this whip in your right hand, with the lash pointing backward, enter the stable alone. It is a great disadvantage in training a horse to have any one in the stable with you; you should be entirely alone, so as to have nothing but yourself to attract his attention. If he is wild, you will soon see him on the opposite side of the stable from you; and now is the time to use a little judgment. I should not want, for myself, more than half or three-quarters of an hour to handle any kind of a colt, and have him running about in the stable after me; though I would advise a new beginner to take more time, and not be in too much of a hurry. If you have but one colt to gentle, and are not particular about the length of time you spend, and have not had any experience in handling colts, I would advise you to take Mr. Powel's method at first, till you gentle him, which he says takes from two to six hours. But as I want to accomplish the same, and what is more, teach the horse to lead, in less than one hour, I shall give you a much quicker process of accomplishing the same end. Accordingly, when you have entered the stable, stand still, and let your horse look at you a minute or two, and as soon as he is settled in one place, approach him slowly, with both arms stationary, your right hanging by your side, holding the whip as directed and the left bent at the elbow, with your hand projecting. As you approach him, go not too much towards his head or croup, so as not to make him move either forward or backward, thus keeping your horse stationary; if he does move a little either forward or backward, step a little to the right or left very cautiously; this will keep him in one place. As you get very near him, draw a little to his shoulder, and stop a few seconds. If you are in his reach he will turn his head and smell your hand, not that he has any preference for your hand, but because that is projecting, and is the nearest portion of your body to the horse. This all colts will do, and they will smell your naked hand just as quickly as they will anything that you can put in it, and with just as good an effect, however much some men have preached the doctrine of taming horses by giving them the scent of articles from the hand. I have already proved that to be a mistake. As soon as he touches his nose to your hand, caress him as before directed, always using a very light soft hand, merely touching the horse, always rubbing the way the hair lies, so that your hand will pass along as smoothly as possible. As you stand by his side, you may find it more convenient to rub his neck or the side of his head, which will answer the same purpose as rubbing his forehead. Favour every inclination of the horse to smell or touch you with his nose. Always follow each touch or communication of this kind with the most tender and affectionatc caresses, accompanied with a kind look, and pleasant word of some sort, such as ," Ho! my little boy—ho! my little boy!" "Pretty boy!" "Nice lady!" or something of that kind, constantly repeating the same words, with the same kind, steady tone of voice; for the horse soon learns to read the expression of the face and voice, and will know as well when fear, love, or anger prevails, as you know your own feelings; two of which, fear and anger, a good horseman should never feel.

HOW TO PROCEED IF YOUR HORSE BE OF A STUBBORN DISPOSITION.

If your horse, instead of being wild, seems to be of a stubborn or mulish disposition; if he lays back his ears as you approach him, or turns his heels to kick you, he has not that regard or fear of man that he should have, to enable you to handle him quickly and easily; and it might be well to give him a few sharp cuts with the whip, about the legs, pretty close to the body. It will crack keenly as

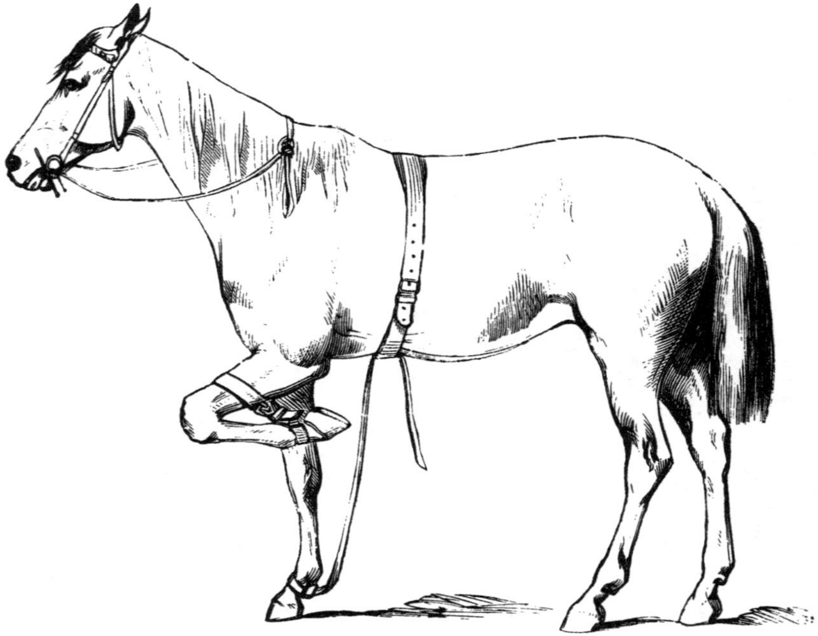

HORSE WITH MR. RAREY'S EXTRA STRAP ON.

it plies around his legs, and the crack of the whip will affect him as much as the stroke; besides, one sharp cut about his legs will affect him more than two or three over his back, the skin on the inner part of his legs or about his flank being thinner, more tender, than on his back. But do not whip him much—just enough to scare him; it is not because we want to hurt the horse that we whip him, we only do it to scare that bad disposition out of him. But whatever you do, do quickly, sharply, and with a good deal of fire, but always without anger. If you are going to scare him at all you must do it at once. Never go into a pitched battle with your horse, and whip him until he is mad and will fight you; you had better not touch him at all, for you will establish, instead of fear and regard, feelings of resentment, hatred, and ill-will. It will do him no good, but an injury, to strike a blow, unless you can scare him; but if you succeed in scaring him, you can whip him without making him mad; for fear and anger never exist together in the horse, and as soon as one is visible, you will find that the other has disappeared. As soon as you have frightened him so that he will stand up straight and pay some attention to you, approach him again, and caress him a good deal more than you whipped him, then you will excite the two controlling passions of his nature, love and fear, and then he will love and fear you too, and, as soon as he learns what to do, will obey quickly.

HOW TO HALTER AND LEAD A COLT.

As soon as you have gentled the colt a little, take the halter in your left hand and approach him as before, and on the same side that you have gentled him. If he is very timid about your approaching closely to him, you can get up to him quicker by making the whip a part of your arm, and reaching out very gently with the butt-end of it; rubbing him lightly on the neck, all the time getting a little closer, shortening the whip by taking it up in your hand, until you finally get close enough to put your hands on him. If he is inclined to hold his head from you, put the end of the halter-strap around his neck, drop your whip, and draw very gently; he will let his neck give, and you can pull his head to you. Then take hold of that part of the halter which buckles over the top of his head, and pass the long side, or that part which goes into the buckle, under his neck, grasping it on the opposite side with your right hand, letting the first strap loose—the latter will be sufficient to hold his head to you. Lower the halter a little, just enough to get his nose into that part which goes around it; then raise it somewhat, and fasten the top buckle, and you will have it all right. The first time you halter a colt you should stand on the left side, pretty well back to his shoulder, only taking hold of that part of the halter that goes round his neck; then with your two hands about his neck you can hold his head to you, and raise the halter on it without making him dodge by putting your hands about his nose. You should have a long rope or strap ready, and as soon as you have the halter on, attach this to it, so that you can let him walk the length of the stable without letting go of the strap, or without making him pull on the halter, for if you only let him feel the weight of your hand on the halter, and give him rope when he runs from you, he will never rear, pull, or throw himself, yet you will be holding him all the time, and doing more towards gentling him than if you had the power to snub him right up and hold him to one spot; because, he does not know anything about his strength, and if you don't do anything to make him pull, he will never know that he can. In a few minutes you can begin to control him with the halter, then shorten the distance between yourself and the horse by taking up the strap in your hand.

As soon as he will allow you to hold him by a tolerably short strap, and to step up to him without flying back, you can begin to give some idea about leading. But to do this, do not go before and attempt to pull him after you, but commence by pulling him very quietly to one side. He has nothing to brace either side of his neck, and will soon yield to a study, gradual pull of the halter; and as soon as you have pulled him a step or two to one side, step up to him and caress him, and then pull him again, repeating this operation until you can pull him around in every direction, and walk about the stable with him, which you can do in a few minutes, for he will soon think when you have made him step to the right or left a few times, that he is compelled to follow the pull of the halter, not knowing that he has the power to resist your pulling; besides you have handled him so gently that he is not afraid of you, and you always caress him when he comes up to you, and he likes that, and would just as lief follow you as not. And after he has had a few lessons of that kind, if you turn him out in a lot, he will come up to you every opportunity he gets. You should lead him about in the stable some time before you take him out, opening the door, so that he can see out, leading him up to it and back again, and past it. See that there is nothing on the outside to make him jump when you take him out, and as you go out with him, try to make him go very slowly, catching hold of the halter close to the jaw with your left hand, while the right is resting on the top of the neck, holding to his mane. After you are out with him a little while, you can lead him about as you please. Don't let any second person come up to you when you first take him out; a stranger taking hold of the halter would frighten him, and make him run. There should not even be any one standing near him, to attract his attention or scare him. If you are alone, and manage him rightly, it will not require any more force to lead or hold him than it would to manage a broken horse.

HOW TO LEAD A COLT BY THE SIDE OF A BROKEN HORSE.

If you should want to lead your colt by the side of another horse, as is often the case, I would advise you to take your horse into the stable, attach a second strap to the colt's halter, and lead your horse up alongside of him. Then get on the broken horse and take one strap around his breast, under his martingale (if he has any on), holding it in your left hand. This will prevent the colt from getting back too far; besides, you will have more power to hold him with the strap pulling against the horse's breast. The other strap take up in your right hand to prevent him from running ahead; then turn him about a few times in the stable, and if the door is wide enough, ride out with him in that position; if not, take the broken horse out first, and stand his breast up against the door, then lead the colt to the same spot, and take the straps as before directed, one on each side of his neck, then let some one start the colt out, and as he comes out, turn your horse to the left, and you will have them all right. This is the best way to lead a colt; you can manage any kind of colt in this way, without any trouble; for if he tries to run ahead, or pull back, the two straps will bring the horses facing each other, so that you can very easily follow up his movements without doing much holding, and as soon as he stops running backward you are right with him, and all ready to go ahead; and if he gets stubborn and does not want to go, you can remove all his stubbornness by riding your horse against his neck, thus compelling him to turn to the right; and as soon as you have turned him about a few times, he will be willing to go along. The next thing, after you have got through leading him, will be to take him into a stable, and hitch him in such a way as not to have him pull on the halter, and as they are often troublesome to get into a stable the first few times, I will give you some instructions about getting him in.

HOW TO LEAD A COLT INTO THE STABLE AND HITCH HIM WITHOUT HAVING HIM PULL ON THE HALTER.

You should lead the broken horse into the stable first, and get the colt, if you can, to follow in after him. If he refuses to go, step up to him, taking a little stick or switch in your right hand; then take hold of the halter close to his head with your left hand, at the same time reaching over his back with your right arm, so that you can tap him on the opposite side with your switch; bring him up facing the door, tap him lightly with your switch, reaching as far back with it as you can. This tapping, by being pretty well back, and on the opposite side, will drive him ahead, and keep him close to you; then, by giving him the right direction with your left hand you can walk into the stable with him. I have walked colts into the stable in this way in less than a minute, after men had worked at them half an hour, trying to pull them in. If you cannot walk him in at once in this way, turn him about and walk him around in every direction, until you can get him up to the door without pulling at him. Then let him stand a few minutes, keeping his head in the right direction with the halter, and he will walk in in less than ten minutes. Never attempt to pull the colt into the stable; that would make him think at once that it was a dangerous place, and if he was not afraid of it before he would be then. Besides, we do not want him to know anything about pulling on the halter. Colts are often hurt, and sometimes killed, by trying to force them into the stable; and those who attempt to do it in that way go into an up-hill business, when a plain smooth road is before them.

If you want to hitch your colt, put him in a tolerably wide stall, which should not be too long, and should be connected by a bar or something of that kind to the partition behind it; so that, after the colt is in, he cannot get far enough back to take a straight, backward pull on the halter; then, by hitching him in the centre of the stall, it would be impossible for him to pull on the halter, the partition behind preventing him from going back, and the halter in the centre checking him every time he turns to the right or left. In a stall of this kind you can break any horse to stand hitched by a light strap, anywhere, without his ever knowing anything about pulling. But if you have broken your horse to lead, and have learned him the use of the halter (which you should always do before you hitch him to anything), you can hitch him in any kind of a stall, and give him something to eat to keep him up to his place for a few minutes at first, and there is not one colt in fifty that will pull on his halter.

THE KIND OF BIT, AND HOW TO ACCUSTOM A HORSE TO IT.

You should use a large, smooth, snaffle-bit, so as not to hurt his mouth, with a bar to each side, to prevent the bit from pulling through either way. This you should attach to the head-stall of your bridle, and put it on your colt without any reins to it, and let him run loose in a large stable or shed some time, until he becomes a little used to the bit, and will bear it without trying to get it out of his mouth. It would be well, if convenient, to repeat this several times, before you do anything more with the colt; as soon as he will bear the bit, attach a single rein to it, without any martingale. You should also have a halter on your colt, or a bridle made after the fashion of a halter, with a strap to it, so that you can hold or lead him about without pulling on the bit much. He is now ready for the saddle.

HOW TO SADDLE A COLT.

Any one man who understands this theory can put a saddle on the wildest colt that ever grew, without any help, and without scaring him. The first thing will be to tie each stirrup-strap into a loose knot to make them short, and prevent the stirrups from flying about and hitting him. Then double up the skirts, and take the saddle under your right arm, so as not to frighten him with it as you approach. When you get to him, rub him gently a few times with your hand, and then raise the saddle very slowly, until he can see it, and smell it, and feel it with his nose. Then let the skirt loose, and rub it very gently against his neck the way the hair lies, letting him hear the rattle of the skirts as he feels them against him—each time getting a little farther backward, and finally slip it over his shoulders on his back. Shake it a little with your hand, and in less than five minutes you can rattle it about over his back as much as you please, and pull it off and throw it on again, without his paying much attention to it.

As soon as you have accustomed him to the saddle, fasten the girth. Be careful how you do this. It often frightens the colt when he feels the girth binding him, and making the saddle fit tight on his back. You should bring up the girth very gently, and not draw it too tight at first, just enough to hold the saddle on. Move him a little, and then girth it as tight as you choose, and he will not mind it.

You should see that the pad of your saddle is all right before you put it on, and that there is nothing to make it hurt him, or feel unpleasant to his back. It should not have any loose straps on the back part of it, to flap about and scare him. After you have saddled him in this way, take a switch in your right hand to tap him up with, and walk about in the stable a few times with your right arm over your saddle, taking hold of the reins on each side of his neck with your right and left hands, thus marching him about in the stable until you teach him the use of the bridle, and can turn him about in any direction, and stop him by a gentle pull of the rein. Always caress him, and loose the reins a little every time you stop him.

You should always be alone, and have your colt in some light stable or shed the first time you ride him; the loft should be high, so that you can sit on his back without endangering your head. You can teach him more in two hours' time in a stable of this kind than you could in two weeks in the common way of breaking colts, out in an open place. If you follow my course of treatment, you need not run any risk, or have any trouble in riding the worst kind of horse. You take him a step at a time, until you get up a mutual confidence and trust between yourself and horse. First teach him to lead and stand hitched; next acquaint him with the saddle and the use of the bit; and then, all that remains is, to get on him without scaring him, and you can ride him as well as any horse.

HOW TO MOUNT THE COLT.

First gentle him well on both sides, about the saddle, and all over, until he will stand still without holding, and is not afraid to see you anywhere about him.

As soon as you have him thus gentled, get a small block, about one foot or eighteen inches in height, and set it down by the side of him, about where you want to stand to mount him; step up on this, raising yourself very gently: horses notice every change of position very closely, and if you were to step up suddenly on the block, it would be very apt to scare him; but, by raising yourself gradually on it, he will see you, without being frightened, in a position very nearly the same as when you are on his back.

As soon as he will bear this without alarm, untie the stirrup-strap next to you, and put your left foot into the stirrup, and stand square over it, holding your knee against the horse, and your toe out, so as to touch him under the shoulder with the toe of your boot. Place your right hand on the front of the saddle, and on the opposite side of you, taking hold of a portion of the mane and the reins, as they hang loosely over his neck, with your left hand; then gradually bear your weight on the stirrup, and on your right hand, until the horse feels your whole weight on the saddle: repeat this several times, each time raising yourself a little higher from the block, until he will allow you to raise your leg over his croup and place yourself in the saddle.

There are three great advantages in having a block to mount from. First, a sudden change of position is very apt to frighten a young horse who has never been handled: he will allow you to walk up to him, and stand by his side, without scaring at you, because you have gentled him to that position; but if you get down on your hands and knees, and crawl towards him, he will be very much frightened; and upon the same principle he would be frightened at your new position, if you had the power to hold yourself over his back without touching him. Then the first great advantage of the block is to gradually gentle him to that new position in which he will see you when you ride him.

Secondly, by the process of leaning your weight in the stirrups, and on your hand, you can gradually accustom him to your weight, so as not to frighten him by having him feel it all at once. And, in the third place, the block elevates you so that you will not have to make a spring in order to get on the horse's back, but from it you can gradually raise yourself into the saddle. When you take these precautions, there is no horse so wild but what you can mount him without making him jump. I have tried it on the worst horses that could be found, and have never failed in any case. When mounting, your horse should always stand without being held. A horse is never well broken when he has to be held with a tight rein when mounting; and a colt is never so safe to mount as when you see that assurance of confidence, and absence of fear, which cause him to stand without holding.

HOW TO RIDE THE COLT

When you want him to start, do not touch him on the side with your heel, or do anything to frighten him and make him jump. But speak to him kindly, and if he does not start, pull him a little to the left until he starts, and then let him walk off slowly with the reins loose. Walk him around in the stable a few times until he gets used to the bit, and you can turn him about in every direction, and stop him as you please. It would be well to get on and off a good many times, until he gets perfectly used to it before you take him out of the stable.

After you have trained him in this way, which should not take you more than one or two hours, you can ride him anywhere you choose without ever having him jump or make an effort to throw you.

When you first take him out of the stable, be very gentle with him, as he will feel a little more at liberty to jump or run, and be a little easier frightened than he was while in the stable. But after handling him so much in the stable, he will be pretty well broken, and you will be able to manage him without trouble or danger.

When you first mount him take a little the shortest hold on the left rein, so that if anything frightens him you can prevent him from jumping by pulling his head around to you. This operation of pulling a horse's head round against his side will prevent any horse from jumping ahead, rearing up, or running away. If he is stubborn and will not go, you can make him move by pulling his head round to one side, when whipping would have no effect. And turning him round a few times will make him dizzy, and then by letting him have his head straight, and giving him a little touch with the whip, he will go along without any trouble.

Never use martingales on a colt when you first ride him; every movement of the hand should go right to the bit in the direction in which it is applied to the reins, without a martingale to change the direction of the force applied. You can guide the colt much better without it, and teach him the use of the bit in much less time. Besides, martingales would prevent you from pulling his head round if he should try to jump.

After your colt has been ridden until he is gentle and well accustomed to the bit, you may find it an advantage if he carries his head too high, or his nose too far out, to put martingales on him.

You should be careful not to ride your colt so far at first as to heat, worry, or tire him. Get off as soon as you see he is a little fatigued; gentle him and let him rest; this will make him kind to you and prevent him from getting stubborn or mad.

THE PROPER WAY TO BIT A COLT.

Farmers often put bitting harnesss on a colt the first thing they do to him, buckling up the bitting as tight as they can draw it, to make him carry his head high, and then turn him out in a field to run a half-day at a time. This is one of the worst punishments that they could inflict on the colt, and very injurious to a young horse that has been used to running in pasture with his head down. I have seen colts so injured in this way that they never got over it.

A horse should be well accustomed to the bit before you put on the bitting harness, and when you first bit him you should only rein his head up to that point where he naturally holds it, let that be high or low; he will soon learn that he cannot lower his head, and that raising it a little will loosen the bit in his mouth. This will give him the idea of raising his head to loosen the bit, and then you can draw the bitting a little tighter every time you put it on, and he will still raise his head to loosen it; by this means you will gradually get his head and neck in the position you want him to carry it, and give him a nice and graceful carriage without hurting him, making him mad, or causing his mouth to get sore.

If you put the bitting on very tight the first time, he cannot raise his head enough to loosen it, but will bear on it all the time, and paw, sweat, and throw himself. Many horses have been killed by falling backward with the bitting on; their heads being drawn up strike the ground with the whole weight of the body. Horses that have their heads drawn up tightly should not have the bitting on more than fifteen or twenty minutes at a time.

HOW TO DRIVE A HORSE THAT IS VERY WILD AND HAS ANY VICIOUS HABITS.

Take up one fore foot and bend his knee till his hoof is bottom upwards, and nearly touching his body; then slip a loop over his knee, and up until it comes above the pastern joint, to keep it up, being careful to draw the loop together between the hoof and pastern joint with a second strap of some kind to prevent the loop from slipping down and coming off. This will leave the horse standing on three legs; you can now handle him as you wish, for it is utterly impossible for him to kick in this position. There is something in this operation of taking up one foot that conquers a horse quicker and better than anything else you can do to him. There is no process in the world equal to it to break a kicking horse, for several reasons. First, there is a principle of this kind in the nature of the horse: that by conquering one member you conquer to a great extent the whole horse.

You have perhaps seen men operate upon this principle, by sewing a horse's ears together to prevent him from kicking. I once saw a plan given in a newspaper to make a bad horse stand to be shod, which was to fasten down one ear. There were no reasons given why you should do so; but I tried it several times, and thought that it had a good effect—though I would not recommend its use; especially stitching his ears together. The only benefit arising from this process is, that by disarranging his ears we draw his attention to them, and he is not so apt to resist the shoeing. By tying up one foot we operate on the same principle to a much better effect. When you first fasten up a horse's foot he will sometimes get very mad, and strike with his knee, and try every possible way to get it down; but he cannot do that, and will soon give up.

This will conquer him better than anything you could do, and without any possible danger of hurting himself or you either, for you can tie up his foot and sit down and look at him until he gives up. When you find that he is conquered, go to him, let down his foot, rub his leg with your hand, caress him, and let him rest a little; then put it up again. Repeat this a few times, always putting up the same foot, and he will soon learn to travel on three legs so that you can drive him some distance. As soon as he gets a little used to this way of travelling, put on your harness, and hitch him to a sulky. If he is the worst kicking horse that ever raised a foot, you need not be fearful of his doing any damage while he has one foot up, for he cannot kick, neither can he run fast enough to do any harm. And if he is the wildest horse that ever had harness on, and has run away every time he has been hitched, you can now hitch him in a sulky, and drive him as you please. If he wants to run, you can let him have the lines, and the whip too, with perfect safety, for he can go but a slow gait on three legs, and will soon be tired, and willing to stop; only hold him enough to guide him in the right direction, and he will soon be tired and willing to stop at the word. Thus you will effectually cure him at once of any further notion of running off. Kicking horses have always been the dread of everybody; you always hear men say, when they speak about a bad horse, "I don't care what he does, so he don't kick." This new method is an effectual cure for this worst of all habits. There are plenty of ways by which you can hitch a kicking horse, and force him to go, though he kicks all the time; but this don't have any good effect towards breaking him, for we know that horses kick because they are afraid of what is behind them, and when they kick against it and it hurts them they will only kick the harder; and this will hurt them still more and make them remember the scrape much longer, and make it still more difficult to persuade them to have any confidence in anything dragging behind them ever after.

But by this new method you can hitch them to a rattling sulky, plough, wagon, or anything else in its worst shape. They may be frightened at first, but cannot kick or do anything to hurt themselves, and will soon find that you do not intend to hurt them, and then they will not care anything more about it. You can then let down the leg and drive along gently without any further trouble. By this new process a bad kicking horse can be learned to go gently in harness in a few hours' time.

ON BALKING.

Horses know nothing about balking, only as they are brought into it by improper management, and when a horse balks in harness it is generally from some mismanagement, excitement, confusion, or from not knowing how to pull, but seldom from any unwillingness to perform all that he understands. High-spirited, free-going horses are the most subject to balking, and only so because drivers do not properly understand how to manage this kind. A free horse in a team may be so anxious to go, that when he hears the word he will start with a jump, which will not move the load, but give him such a severe jerk on the shoulders that he will fly back and stop the other horse; the teamster will continue his driving without any cessation, and by the time he has the slow horse started again he will find that the free horse has made another jump, and again flown back; and now he has them both badly balked, and so confused that neither of them knows what is the matter, or how to start the load. Next will come the slashing and cracking of the whip, and hallooing of the driver, till something is broken or he is through with his course of treatment. But what a mistake the driver commits by whipping his horse for this act! Reason and common sense should teach him that the horse is willing and anxious to go, but did not know how to start the load. And should he whip him for that? If so, he should whip him again for not knowing how to talk. A man that wants to act with any rationality or reason should not fly into a passion, but should always think before he strikes. It takes a steady pressure against the collar to move a load, and you cannot expect him to act with a steady, determined purpose while you are whipping him. There is hardly one balking horse in five hundred that will pull true from whipping; it is only adding fuel to fire, and will make him more liable to balk another time. You always see horses that have been balked a few times, turn their heads and look back, as soon as they are a little frustrated. This is because they have been whipped and are afraid of what is behind them. This is an invariable rule with balked horses, just as much as it is for them to look around at their sides when they have the bots; in either case they are deserving of the same sympathy and the same kind, rational treatment.

When your horse balks or is a little excited, if he

wants to start quickly, or looks around and doesn't want to go—there is something wrong, and he needs kind treatment immediately. Caress him kindly, and if he doesn't understand at once what you want him to do, he will not be so much excited as to jump and break things, and do everything wrong through fear. As long as you are calm, and keep down the excitement of the horse, there are ten chances to have him understand you, where there would not be one under harsh treatment, and then the little flare up would not carry with it any unfavorable recollections, and he would soon forget all about it, and learn to pull true. Almost every wrong act the horse commits is from mismanagement, fear, or excitement; one harsh word will so excite a nervous horse as to increase his pulse ten beats in a minute.

When we remember that we are dealing with dumb brutes, and reflect how difficult it must be for them to understand our motions, signs, and language, we should never get out of patience with them because they don't understand us, or wonder at their doing things wrong. With all our intellect, if we were placed in the horse's situation, it would be difficult for us to understand the driving of some foreigner, of foreign ways and foreign language. We should always recollect that our ways and language are just as foreign and unknown to the horse as any language in the world is to us, and should try to practise what we could understand were we the horse, endeavoring by some simple means to work on his understanding rather than on the different parts of his body. All balked horses can be started true and steady in a few minutes' time; they are all willing to pull as soon as they know how, and I never yet found a balked horse that I could not teach to start his load in fifteen, and often less than three, minutes' time.

Almost any team, when first balked, will start kindly if you let them stand five or ten minutes as though there was nothing wrong, and then speak to them with a steady voice, and turn them a little to the right or left, so as to get them both in motion before they feel the pinch of the load. But if you want to start a team that you are not driving yourself, that has been balked, fooled and whipped for some time, go to them and hang the lines on their hames, or fasten them to the wagon, so that they will be perfectly loose; make the drivver and spectators (if there are any) stand off some distance to one side, so as not to attract the attention of the horse; unloose their check-reins, so that they can get their heads down if they choose; let them stand, a few minutes in this condition until you can see that they are a little composed. While they are standing you should be about their heads, gentling them; it will make them a little more kind, and the spectators will think that you are doing something that they do not understand, and will not learn the secret. When you have them ready to start, stand before them, and as you seldom have but one balky horse in a team, get as near in front of him as you can, and if he is too fast for the other horse, let his nose come against your breast; this will keep him steady, for he will go slow rather than run on you; turn them gently to the right, without letting them pull on the traces as far as the tongue will let them go; stop them with a kind word, gentle them a little, and then turn them back to the left, by the same process. You will have them under your control by this time, and as you turn them again to the right, steady them in the collar, and you can take them where you please.

There is a quicker process that will generally start a balky horse, but not so sure. Stand him a little ahead, so that his shoulders will be against the collar, and then take up one of his forefeet in your hand, and let the driver start them, and when the weight comes against his shoulders, he will try to step; then let him have his foot, and he will go right along. If you want to break a horse from balking that has long been in that habit, you ought to set apart a half-day for that purpose. Put him by the side of some steady horse; have check-lines on them; tie up all the traces and straps, so that there will be nothing to excite them; do not rein them up, but let them have their heads loose. Walk them about together for some time as slowly and lazily as possible; stop often, and go up to your balky horse and gentle him. Do not take any whip about him, or do anything to excite him, but keep him just as quiet as you can. He will soon learn to start off at the word, and stop whenever you tell him.

As soon as he performs rightly, hitch him in an empty wagon; have it stand in a favorable position for starting. It would be well to shorten the stay-chain behind the steady horse, so that if it is necessary, he can take the weight of the wagon the first time you start them. Do not drive but a few rods at first; watch your balky horse closely, and if you see that he is getting excited, stop him before he stops of his own accord, caress him a little, and start again. As soon as they go well, drive them over a small hill a few times, and then over a larger one, occasionally adding a little load.

This process will make any horse true to pull.

TO BREAK A HORSE TO HARNESS.

Take him in a light stable, as you did to ride him; take the harness and go through the same process that you did with the saddle, until you get him familiar with it, so that you can put it on him, and rattle it about without his caring for it. As soon as he will bear this, put on the lines, caress him as you draw them over him, and drive him about in the stable till he will bear them over his hips. The lines are a great aggravation to some colts, and often frighten them as much as if you were to raise a whip over them. As soon as he is familiar with the harness and lines, take him out and put him by the side of a gentle horse, and go through the same process that you did with the balking horse. Always use a bridle without blinds when you are breaking a horse to harness.

HOW TO HITCH A HORSE IN A SULKY.

Lead him to and around it; let him look at it, touch it with his nose, and stand by it till he does not care for it; then pull the shafts a little to the left, and stand your horse in front of the off-wheel. Let some one stand on the right side of the horse, and hold him by the bit, while you stand on the left side, facing the sulky. This will keep him straight. Run your left hand back, and let it rest on his hip, and lay hold of the shafts with your right, bringing them up very gently to the left hand, which still remains stationary. Do not let anything but your arm touch his back, and as soon as you have the shafts square over him, let the person on the opposite side take hold of one of them, and lower them very gently to the shaft-bearers. Be very slow and deliberate about hitching; the longer time you take the better, as a general thing. When you have the shafts placed, shake them slightly, so that he will feel them against each side. As soon as he will bear them without scaring, fasten your braces, &c., and start him along very slowly. Let one man lead the horse, to keep him gentle, while the other gradually works back with the lines till he can get behind and drive him. After you have driven him in this way a short distance, you can get into the sulky, and all will go right. It is very important to have your horse go gently when you first hitch him. After you have walked him awhile, there is not half so much danger of his scaring. Men do very wrong to jump up behind a horse to drive him as soon as they have him hitched. There are too many things for him to comprehend all at once. The shafts, the lines, the harness, and the rattling of the sulky, all tend to scare him, and he must be made familiar with them by degrees. If your horse is very wild, I would advise you to put up one foot the first time you drive him.

HOW TO MAKE A HORSE LIE DOWN.

Everything that we want to teach the horse must be commenced in some way to give him an idea of what you want him to do, and then be repeated till he learns it perfectly. To make a horse lie down, bend his left fore leg and slip a loop over it, so that he cannot get it down. Then put a surcingle around his body, and fasten one end of a long strap around the other fore leg, just above the hoof. Place the other end under the surcingle, so as to keep the strap in the right direction; take a short hold of it with your right hand; stand on the left side of the horse, grasp the bit in your left hand, pull steadily on the strap with your right; bear against his shoulder till you cause him to move. As soon as he lifts his weight, your pulling will raise the other foot, and he will have to come on his knees. Keep the strap tight in your hand, so that he cannot straighten his leg if he rises up. Hold him in this position, and turn his head towards you; bear against his side with your shoulder, not hard, but with a steady, equal pressure, and in about ten minutes he will lie down. As soon as he lies down, he will be completely conquered, and you can handle him as you please. Take off the straps, and straighten out his legs; rub him lightly about the face and neck with your hand the way the hair lies; handle all his legs, and after he has lain ten or twenty minutes, let him get up again. After resting him a short time make him lie down as before. Repeat the operation three or four times, which will be sufficient for one lesson. Give him two lessons a day, and when you have given him four lessons, he will lie down by taking hold of one foot. As soon as he is well broken to lie down in this way, tap him on the opposite leg with a stick when you take hold of his foot, and in a few days he will lie down from the mere motion of the stick.

HOW TO MAKE A HORSE FOLLOW YOU.

Turn him into a large stable or shed, where there is no chance to get out, with a halter or bridle on. Go to him and gentle him a little, take hold of his halter and turn him towards you, at the same time touching him lightly over the hips with a long whip. Lead him the length of the stable, rubbing him on the neck, saying in a steady tone of voice as you lead him, "Come along boy?" or use his name instead of "boy" if you choose. Every time you turn touch him slightly with the whip, to make him step up close to you, and then caress him with your hand. He will soon learn to hurry up to escape the whip and be caressed, and you can make him follow you around without taking hold of the halter. If he should stop and turn from you, give him a few sharp cuts about the hind legs, and he will soon turn his head towards you, when you must always caress him. A few lessons of this kind will make him run after you, when he sees the motion of the whip—in twenty or thirty minutes he will follow you about the stable. After you have given him two or three lessons in the stable, take him out into a small field and train him; and from thence you can take him into the road and make him follow you anywhere, and run after you.

HOW TO MAKE A HORSE STAND WITHOUT HOLDING.

After you have him well broken to follow you, place him in the centre of the stable—begin at his head to caress him, gradually working backwards. If he moves, give him a cut with the whip, and put him back to the same spot from which he started. If he stands, caress him as before, and continue gentling him in this way until you can get round him without making him move. Keep walking around him, increasing your pace, and only touch him occasionally. Enlarge your circle as you walk around, and if he then moves, give him another cut with the whip, and put him back to his place. If he stands, go to him frequently and caress him, and then walk around him again. Do not keep him in one position too long at a time, but make him come to you occasionally, and follow you around the stable. Then make him stand in another place, and proceed as before. You should not train your horse more than half an hour at a time.

www.ingramcontent.com/pod-product-compliance
Lightning Source LLC
LaVergne TN
LVHW011235110826
845150LV00006B/1644